Backyard Food Security for the Common Person

The Ignored Resource

By Josh and Ashlee Kirschner
Co-authored by Jamie Giesbrecht

Backyard Food Security for the Common Person

The Ignored Resource

Cover Design by: Josh and Ashlee Kirschner
Cover Photos by: Jamie Giesbrecht and Ashlee Kirschner

By Josh Kirschner, Ashlee Kirschner and Jamie Giesbrecht

Published: by ashlee kirschner

ISBN: 978-1-9990102-2-5
ISBN: 978-1-9990102-3-2
Copyright © 2020 by ashlee kirschner

All rights reserved. No part of this publication may be reproduced, distributed, or transmitted in any form or by any means, including photocopying, recording, or other electronic or mechanical methods, without the prior written permission of the publisher, except in the case of brief quotations embodied in critical reviews and certain other noncommercial uses permitted by copyright law.

Introduction	3
Seed Starting	7
Helping Your Plants Grow	23
What Should I Grow?	31
Taking the Chickens to Town	39
Bringing the Bees to Town	53
Making Your Yard Work for You	59
Supplementing Your Yard	68
Foraging, Hunting and Fishing	68
Making Your Abundance Last	81
Buying with Food Security in Mind	94
Conclusion	103
Bonus Chapter	105
Beyond the Basics of the Backyard	105

Introduction

With the world in recent chaos because of the unfolding Coronavirus pandemic, the desire, scratch that, the necessity of growing in our yards has become apparent. While we have often used our backyards as storage, a place for flowers and foliage or even nothing at all, the potential for growing an abundance of food is literally within our fingertips. Though not difficult, it is so often neglected. Maybe it is neglected through misconceptions about the effort and the prior knowledge needed. Or maybe it is neglected because it's simply so much easier to go to the grocery store.

If the upheaval and supermarket shortages have shown us anything, they have shown us how very inadequately we are prepared. It should have shown us how our laziness in making our own food security a priority is affecting our mental health.

Maybe you can't grow enough food to last an entire year. But you absolutely can grow enough produce to heavily supplement your needs throughout the entire year. In most municipalities, you can raise chickens or have bees that will again supplement how greatly you rely on a market that can, as we now see, rapidly change. You can hunt and forage.

YOU CAN DO SOMETHING ABOUT YOUR OWN FOOD SECURITY. YOU DO NOT NEED TO BE COMPLETELY THROWN AROUND BY THE ECONOMY.

Guys, you, literally have so much potential sitting in your backyard. We cannot even contain how excited we get looking in our tiny backyard and seeing how much it can do for our family. Our yards, small or large, have so much potential to be incredibly useful - to bring a level of security unparallelled into the daily struggle of providing food for our families.

And let's stray from food security for just a moment. Growing food is not only good for providing security, it's also beneficial for your mental and physical health (because you're eating healthier, getting exercise and spending more time outdoors). By growing your own food, you encourage more beneficial insects and wildlife to come make a home in your neighbourhood. And by adding more trees, you start adding more plants that release oxygen and absorb carbon dioxide - literally helping deal with air pollution one tree at a time. I could list the benefits for ages upon ages because there are so many.

Although still perfecting, we are learning the tools to live more and more self-sufficiently every day. Our (Josh and Ashlee's) family of six lives in about a 900 square foot house on 0.17 of an acre. On this property (which we are realizing can give us much more produce than it already has been), we have six chickens, five fruit trees, twelve fruit bushes, two fruiting vines and oodles of strawberries, all nestled between gardens of herbs, vegetables and annual fruits. AND we are confident we have the potential to grow nearly double what we are currently at.

Last year, we canned approximately 220 jars (I eventually lost count) of produce from our garden, things we foraged from the forest and town and produce we bought in bulk and in season. We dried enough herbs to last almost the entire fall and winter and spring (so nearly until we were ready to plant again). We filled our freezers with pumpkin, kale, cabbage and fruit. We connected with our friends and they raised meat chickens on their property which we butchered together.

And all of this we did in a zone two region. That means we live in an area where winter temperatures can get down to -40 degrees Celsius (even colder sometimes). And we know we can do more. We're hoping to get bees and maybe meat rabbits this summer and add significantly to the growing space in our yard. We know we can grow far more than we already are, we simply need to cultivate more wasted yard space into growing space. The room is there, we merely need to harness its potential.

Seed Starting

We have one goal with this book: to make you realize how simple growing your own food can be. Starting seeds is SIMPLE.

However, with that in mind, we want you to grow food. If you find starting seeds to be too tedious or time consuming, go to a nursery and buy vegetable plant starts. When we first started growing our own food, our seeds often died and it just seemed like we could not get things to grow. So we gave up and bought plants from the nursery. We did that for a couple of years until we realized we were spending way more money than we had to. If we could simply master the art of growing seeds, we could save ourselves oodles of money. And this was too enticing for an overly practical person to ignore. So we started learning to start almost everything from seed.

If you find starting seeds to be too tedious or time consuming, go to a nursery and buy vegetable plant starts.

Before we get too far into this chapter, realize there are many ways to grow seeds. There are different theories on what is best and how to best do things. However, our goal is simplicity. We want you to see how easy it is to grow food. So, we are going to tell you about the simplest methods we've found to work (and the methods that have cost us the least).

There are seven keys to starting your seeds and getting them to grow well.

1. Read the seed package
2. Get a good growing medium
3. Make sure your seedlings have enough light
4. Keep the seedlings warm
5. Thin the seeds (boohoo)
6. Don't overwater them
7. Prepare them for their lives outdoors

That's it. Those are our keys for growing seedlings well. And simply for the sake of clarity, let's go into each of these keys with a bit more detail.

1. Read the seed package

Whenever you buy a package of seeds, you will find a fountain of information on the back of the package. This information really tells you everything you need to know ... really. It will tell you if and when you need to start your seeds indoors (for instance four to six weeks before the last frost day (up here in our zone two climate our last frost day is usually right around May Long weekend)) or if you can simply put them right in the ground. It will tell you when your seedling is ready to go outside, what kind of conditions to plant in (full sun, shade, sandy soil, etc.) and when it's ready to harvest. It will even tell you if your seed needs any extra care before planting it (such as soaking the seeds in water before planting).

Most everything you need to know about starting plants from seed is right on that package. All you have to do is READ IT.

2. Get a good growing medium

We have found this point to be a game changer in our seed growing experience. But before I tell you about this, let me define my term. What exactly is a "growing medium?" A "growing medium" is whatever you happen to be growing your seeds in. So your growing medium can be dirt, water (this would be for hydroponic growing), sand, a mixture of things or really anything you find that you can get a plant to grow in.

So now that we're set on terms, let's figure out what kind of growing medium a seed needs. A seed needs light and airy soil. They will not grow in clay (and if they do, you have a super seed so good for you). They will not grow in sand. They need something somewhere in between glue and straight sand. We have found getting seed starter potting soil (which is <u>NOT</u> the same as regular potting soil) works well OR we make our own mix. This mix includes peat moss (I know, it's not a renewable resource. I know, we need to find something different than peat moss. We just haven't yet. We will. I promise), vermiculite, perlite and worm castings.

3. Make sure your seedlings have enough light

This point is essential. If your plants do not get enough light they will die. You can buy a grow light if you want, but we have found a grow light is not essential to growing seeds well. They simply need adequate sunlight.

Take a look at your house and figure out how it is situated. Which windows are south facing? Find out which windows those are and grow your seedlings in front of those windows. The south facing windows will by far give your plants the most sunlight and will encourage them to thrive from the get go.

In our tiny house, we have two south facing windows. One is above our kitchen sink (so not ideal for putting seedlings) and the other is in our children's bedroom (and that tiny room already houses three children). So again, not ideal for putting a bunch of seedlings. We have opted to put all of our seedlings on a card table in our front window. It's not completely ideal, but it's the best we can do ... and it's working fabulously.

This brings me to point number four,

4. Keep the seedlings warm

This is another crucial aspect of getting your plants to grow well. Again, if you want, you can go and buy a seed warming tray. I am sure they work wonderfully. But we are a large family and our budget is tight so we've never done this.

As mentioned in the previous point, our seedlings are on a card table in front of our front window. This card table just happens to be situated directly beside a heat vent. That heat vent and the sunlight has been completely adequate in keeping our seedlings happy and growing well. That's it. No fancy contraptions. Just the heat vent, the window and a card table.

5. Thin the seeds (boohoo)

After you have everything set up for your seeds, you need to plant them. We like to plant small seeds in a six-celled starter tray like this.

We do reuse these trays over and over (until the plastic is so worn out, they rip apart when you pick them up). You can also use coconut coir pots (in theory, they are supposed to compost in the ground as your plant is growing, but this doesn't happen very quickly - like I've found them in the dirt at harvest time not decomposed at all) or cardboard pots (which start decomposing little by little every time you water your seeds). We like using the plastic starter trays, partly because they are a bit easier to work with and partly because we always have an abundance from the work we do with our landscaping company.

Because we are reusing plastic trays, we have found we MUST clean the trays thoroughly before reusing them (we clean them in the sink or bathtub with hot water and dish soap). Sometimes some of the seeds from last year had an issue (like they got a disease, bugs, etc.) so it is absolutely imperative all the trays get a good clean before sticking vulnerable, new seeds in them.

Once your pots are ready and filled with a good growing medium, you need to plant your seeds. Many seeds are small - micro small - like you can barely see them small. Because of this, you will end up putting multiple seeds in each cell.

- *Helpful Note* - We also put two to three bigger seeds (ones that are big enough to hold between two fingers) in each cell (so the likelihood of something growing is higher.)

A handful of radicchio seeds (carrot seeds are even smaller than this).

You wait and then you finally see little seedlings starting to emerge. And you're so excited ... but you realize you have a problem - there are way too many seedlings growing in a much too small space.

You have been forced into doing something terribly difficult. You must pull out all of the weaker plants, leaving only the one, strongest plant in each cell. The fancy plant word for this process is called thinning. And it is awful. I hate it. I make Josh do it.

Sometimes we don't do it because I hate - hate - pulling perfectly fine, but smaller little plants out. But whenever we refuse to thin, all the seedlings, both strong and weak, are encumbered from ever growing to their full potential.

Let me give you an example. A few years ago, I just could not bear thinning my carrots. There were so many little carrot tops coming up in the row and it was so beautiful and I was so proud of them and I knew I should thin them, but I simply wouldn't because it made me so sad. But when it came to harvest time, what we pulled up was pitiful. If there even were any carrots (sometimes there was such a lack of space they didn't grow at all), they were miniscule or twisted around another carrot. The entire crop was mostly a waste because I was not harsh enough to thin.

I know it is awful, but this is something you must do. You have to thin your seedlings.

One more quick note: When we plant squash seeds, we usually plant them in a pot like this.

Squash seeds are large and the seedlings they become are also large. They outgrow a six-cell seedling tray incredibly fast. So, we just skip a step and plant them right into a pot.

6. Don't overwater them

This is a common problem for many seedling parents. They want to make sure their plants are thriving and so they water them over and over. But what these overanxious parents don't realize is they are drowning their seedlings. Drowning them.

We have absolutely one hundred percent had this happen. When we have overwatered, the seedlings usually damp off (fancy plant talk for the root rotted and the plant died).

In our house, Josh has become the sole waterer. That means there is no doubling on watering and a strict, seemingly callous, watering schedule is kept. And when I say water, what I really mean is mist. We have a spray bottle that Josh mists the seeds with. After the seeds have developed into actual plants, Josh starts watering with a typical watering can.

Josh ends up watering the seedlings about every two to three days. However, he checks the seedlings and growing medium daily - if it is bone dry they need to be watered a bit more often. He needs to water the seedlings more frequently when they start growing bigger and using the water quicker, but it is still done on a strict schedule.

> *- Before We Forget, A Note on Transplanting (or moving seedlings into bigger pots) -*

If you live in a Northern climate like we do, you may have to keep your seedlings in pots in a greenhouse or in your house for a fairly long time before it is warm enough to plant them outside. I know it gets difficult to wait (especially when you get a handful of warm days in a row), but you need to make sure to wait until the last frost day to plant outside (again, in my region that day is right around May Long weekend). If you get ancy and plant them too soon, you may kill everything. Me and Josh did that one year and EVERYTHING - every single one of our plants - died in a just below freezing night. Don't do that.

While you are waiting for that last frost day to come, you may notice some of your seedlings are outgrowing their six-cell tray. According to Monty Don (if you are British, you will understand this reference. If you are not British, Monty Don is the best gardener of all time - other names he is known by are, "King of Horticulture," or "Head Gardener of England."), you can tell a plant has outgrown its current cell or pot when the roots start coming out the bottom.

Like this →

But now you run into an issue. If it is not yet warm enough to plant outside, you cannot leave the plants where they are, but you cannot plant them in the ground. So you will have to transplant those seedlings, or rather put them in a bigger pot.

It is a little scary transplanting small seedlings. But it's not that bad. If you view the seedlings as being fragile, you will treat them gently and most likely everything will be fine. The things you most need to watch for are:

1. Making sure the plant is transplanted into its new home with all of its root mass (if it doesn't have its roots, it will die - same goes for every plant ever).
2. And making sure you don't snap the plant in half as you pull it out of the cell.

Josh says I am aggressive, reckless and rough when transplanting our seedlings (but they survive so ... so there. (Josh will tell you how he transplants below)). I usually tip the six-cell seed tray upside down, keep one hand over the other seedlings (so they don't fall out of the tray) and squeeze the bottom of one cell so the root mass loosens and that particular seedling comes out.

We let these Sweet Williams stay in their pot for WAY too long. Our oldest daughter planted these seeds in the fall and we overwintered them in the window in our bathroom.

Here you see me removing them from the seeding tray.

Now that the seedling is out of the tray, I am gently pulling apart the roots to separate the plants.

After the seedling is out of the cell, I somewhat gently (aggressively according to Josh) put it into a bigger pot with dirt. See the pictures below.

Putting the plant into its own pot

The finished product.

    I (Josh) take a slightly less aggressive approach when transplanting seedlings. Holding the seedlings upright (like God intended) I prefer to gently squeeze the sides of the seedling cell until the roots and growing

17

medium loosen and pull away from the sides of the cell. I then push up from the bottom, while supporting the stem, until the seedling pops out.

I place it into the already prepared planting hole, backfill around the seedling with dirt, and then gently but firmly "firm in" the plant by pressing the dirt down around it.

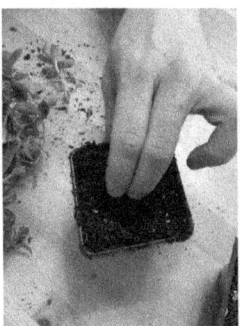
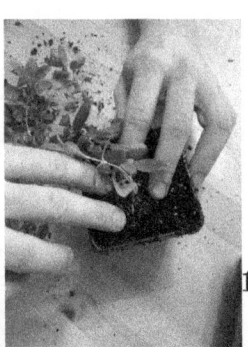

7. Prepare them for their lives outdoors

You're so close to getting your plants growing in those garden beds. The seedlings are healthy and strong and the days are getting warmer and warmer. You pass the last frost day and put all your plants outside expecting they will thrive, but are horrified when they start yellowing and the leaves start curling. What happened?

If your plant goes directly from a pampered life indoors to facing the harsh reality of wind, sun and rain outside, it will go into shock (and sometimes die). Do not be disheartened. There is an incredibly easy solution to this.

While you are waiting for the last frost day to come, you will most definitely have warm days. Start sticking your seedlings outside for short amounts of time on those warm days. Start with a small amount of time (one to two hours) and then bring them back inside. Gradually increase that time until they are outside most of the day. (The plant term for this is called "hardening off your seedlings.") Because your seedlings are babies, they will still need at least some protection from the elements like the wind and sun (make sure it isn't too hot wherever you put them - this can also overwhelm and shock them). If you are certain, it will not go below freezing (if it goes below 0 degrees Celsius, your seedlings will for sure die), you can start keeping your seedlings in a greenhouse overnight.

The main point of this is: gradually prepare your seedlings for a life outdoors. If you do this, they will be adequately prepared and strong enough to handle all the elements when their time comes to live in garden beds.

Seed Problems 101

Here are some problems we've had with seeds.

1. They damp off (or the roots rot)

As stated above, the case for this is usually that we've overwatered. Sometimes there are other factors at play such as disease, etc., but most of the time it's from overwatering. If your seedlings damp off, you just need to throw them away. They will never recover. Sorry.

2. You get aphids or whiteflies (aka bad little bugs)

A common problem with growing food is pesty, bad bugs, such as aphids. Aphids eat away at your plant, poop out a sweet substance and ants harvest it (basically the ants treat the aphids like cattle and bring them from one spot to another (like grazing cattle) on plants. The ants also get quite aggressive when you try to deal with the aphid problem and will bite you ... which actually hurts. All of this is completely unnecessary information for these purposes, but I think it is fascinating so you get to hear me talk about it.) Aphids are hard to deal with - they multiply by the millions (aphids can reproduce sexually or asexually (meaning they can reproduce clones of themselves - isn't that wild??)), but you can deal with them if you are diligent. When you go and check on your seedlings, take a quick look underneath the leaves for aphids (they love the undersides of leaves). If you see them, squish them immediately.

You can also deal with aphids with pesticides. We have a strict no harsh chemical pesticide rule in our household. So even though there are products that will probably get rid of aphids in the flash of an eye, we refuse to use them. We instead either use a concoction made of dish soap (you can find recipes by the dozen on the internet), Safer's Soap (my personal favourite), squish them, spray them off with water or buy and release ladybugs (ladybugs eat aphids like crazy monsters). These techniques are not as quick acting or necessarily as effective as harsh chemicals, but they are safe and that is a much higher priority to us.

Another problem bug that often plagues seedlings is whiteflies - little flying white bugs. A great help for this is using yellow sticky tape traps (you can find these at a nursery or probably any store that sells plants - this is a very common product). The yellow colour attracts the bugs so they fly towards that and end up getting stuck on the tape for the rest of their short lives. However, do not - I repeat, DO NOT - lean down to check on your seedlings while letting your ponytail dangle beside the tape. Your hair will absolutely get stuck in it and it is repulsive and hard to get off and just awful.

Helpful Note - Do not - DO NOT - stick yellow sticky traps in your trees to deal with aphid or other pest bug problems. Yes, it seems like an environmentally friendly idea, but guys, we have had birds get stuck on those traps (twice in one week). It was absolutely traumatizing and made us feel like some of the worst people in the entire world. We realized we could have potentially used the sticky traps if we had cut them into small pieces, but I don't know. The birds' wings still might have caught on them ... ???? Can't think about this anymore. Too traumatizing.

Helping Your Plants Grow

Like the previous chapter, we want to emphasize one thing. Growing your own food is SIMPLE. Yes, you can do one hundred thousand things to make your plants grow well. And yes, everyone has ideas on what works best (and they're often differing), but growing your own food can be SO SIMPLE AND EASY. You don't have to know everything there is to know about plants to grow food well, you just need to know a few things.

One of the best things you can do when first starting to grow plants is find senior citizens in your community who have been (or still are) avid gardeners. These people are by far the best resource you have for figuring out what is going on with your plants and how to deal with issues that arise in your area. It doesn't matter if they don't have horticulture schooling, they have experience and in the plant world (in our opinion), experience trumps book knowledge every time. They know what doesn't work (because they've probably already tried it) and they also know what does work. So find those people and beg them to pass their knowledge on to you. In all likelihood, they will be absolutely delighted and you will get to skip all those hard-growing learning curves they've already gone through.

So although we're not seniors, in our lifetime, we have learned quite a few things that do and do not work. And we're going to share these things with you. We'll break it down like this.

1. *Put the right plant in the right place*
2. *Add goodies in to help your plant thrive*
3. *Take care of your plant*
4. *Try any plant, but give it up if it doesn't work*

Sounds pretty daunting, doesn't it? Let's look at this terrifying list a little closer.

1. Put the right plant in the right place

Before you put any plant in the ground, you need to know that plant. I know this sounds scary, but let me go back to something we covered in the first chapter. You can get to know your plant by

A. reading the seed package
B. reading the tag that comes with the plant from the nursery or
C. if getting the plant from a friend, looking up things about the plant on the internet.

So again, the most basic aspects of a plant's survival are dependent on one thing - **reading the tag.**

Secondly after reading the tag, you need to implement what it says. Does your plant like shade? Put it in a shady spot. Does it want sunlight, find a spot that is sunny for most of the day.

Helpful Note - Most all vegetables and herbs want lots of sun. We've tried growing them in the shade, but besides mint and parsley, none of them seem to like it very much).

Another thing your plant tag will most likely say is the zones your plant will thrive in. Zones are another fancy plant term for grouping which plants thrive in which climates. For instance, an orange will survive in a hot climate (so zone 9-11), while an apple tree needs winter to fruit (so it grows in zones 2-5). If you are growing a plant outside of its natural temperature home, expect that it will either

1. Need to be babied and has a high potential of dying or
2. Die

The last piece of helpful information often given on the tag is the plant's soil preference. Does this plant prefer sandy soil? Does it want the soil to be more acidic? All this information will be found on the tag or on the internet. But before you start worrying about this one too much, let me put your mind at rest.

Plants want soil that is full of nutrients and most want soil that is somewhere between glue like clay and holds-nothing-in-it sand. Having good soil is critical in pushing your plant from living to thriving.

So how do you get good soil? Let's move to point two.

Rhubarb coming up in spring

2. Add goodies in to help your plant thrive

So you want good soil? Guess what the best soil additives are? Animal manure (even including dog poop) and kitchen scraps. Expensive, I know. Chicken, sheep, cow and horse manure (all available in pretty bags from the store (so you can pretend you aren't actually buying poop)) are amazing tools in getting your soil in tip top condition. As for the kitchen scraps, any vegetable and fruit scraps turn into what we call compost. Compost can be made of much other organic material (such as grass clippings, leaves, saw dust, etc.), but if you only use organic kitchen scraps, you will still be ahead.

We have a huge compost pile in our backyard, but whenever we move, we will most likely change things up. Our pile is so huge (we also add all of our yard waste to that pile), it is a pain to deal with. In order for your organic waste material to turn into a garden super weapon, it needs to be turned (so new stuff goes to the bottom, bottom stuff goes to the top, etc.). Our pile gets so large that the idea of turning it is exhausting.

So in the future, we will do one of two things. We will either buy a food composter from the hardware store or we will have three different compost piles (one for woody material, one for kitchen scraps and one for grass, leaves, etc.).

Before I move too far off the topic of compost. I want to put in a quick tidbit about egg shells. Eggshells are another phenomenal super weapon. We save all our egg shells, throw them in the blender and then throw them right in our garden beds. Eggshells help put air pockets in clay soil and they can help protect your plants against slugs and other bothersome critters.

If you really want your plants to thrive, you can also add other goodies in. Having a healthy, nutrient rich soil, is absolutely the best thing you can do for your plants. But if you want to do a bit extra for them, you can add fertilizer every month or so.

Josh and I prefer to use fairly gentle fertilizers (you can get very strong fertilizers which means they most likely have strong chemicals in them). We spread a slow release granular fertilizer over all of our garden beds in the spring which slowly releases nutrients throughout the season. Or we put fruit fertilizer spikes around our trees (these also slowly release nutrients to the tree). We sometimes put fish fertilizer (it is terribly stinky) on our tomatoes. And we ALWAYS put bone meal in our holes whenever we're planting something new. Bone meal helps establish strong roots and hence is a great start to your plant making your yard its new home.

But again, we'll reiterate this. The very best goodie you can add in for your plants' health is compost or manure. Top dress (fancy word for spread a thin layer around) your garden beds and plants with compost and manure often.

3. Take care of your plant

I know this point should go without saying, but I'll say it anyway. Take care of your plant. Here are a few things to note.

Water your plant properly. This means don't underwater your plant and don't overwater it. The rule of thumb is this. Water fewer times, but water deep. So instead of watering your plant for 5 seconds once a day, water your plant two or three times a week for 30 seconds. Doing this will encourage your plant to grow deep and strong roots. And with strong roots, a plant can really withstand almost anything.

Don't plant monocrops. In other words, don't only plant one thing. If you only plant one thing, it is highly likely bugs or disease will ravage your yard and when they do, your whole crop is gone. All your work is undone. Beneficial insects and good soil health depend on plant diversity. Plant different things.

Rotate your crops. Like the previous point, bugs and disease thrive when you plant the same things in the same spot year after year. If you plant potatoes in the same spot every year, don't be surprised if you find your crop being ruined by potato beetles. By moving your crop, you are basically confusing the bad bugs. They don't know where their snacks went and they leave your plants alone. Besides that, different plants use different nutrients in the soil and give off different benefits. So, if you put the same crops in the same spot every year, the soil will be depleted of one nutrient and have too much of another. Simply put - cycle your veggie crops from one garden bed to another (or just another spot in a big garden bed) year to year. We have about a three-year cycle, so the crops that were in one bed ending up being in that same bed about three or four years after they were last there.

Weed your garden beds. Going into your garden and hoeing between the rows every few weeks is so beneficial for your plants. The problem with weeds is that they are basically a super plant - they rapidly self-seed all over the place (so new plants popping up everywhere) and they grow so well that they take over whatever you put in the ground.

If possible, plant disease resistant plants. Some plants, like cucumber, are especially susceptible to getting plant diseases like powdery mildew. Powdery mildew is a plant disease that leaves your plant looking like it has been in a chalk fight. But beyond the unsightly problem, the real issue is powdery mildew slowly kills off your plant.

To be honest, plant diseases are really hard to deal with. Once a plant has a disease, it is spread through water (so rain droplets splattering off one infected leaf to another and so on). There are remedies you can try to do to stop or slow a disease, but it is difficult.

The more you grow things, the more likely you are to recognize which plants in your yard are susceptible to disease. When you see that, go to the nursery and search for new plants that are disease resistant. We look for cucumber seeds or plants that say something like "mildew resistant" on them. It really helps.

4. Try any plant, but give up if it doesn't work

This point is a bit harsh, but it's practical. Josh and I have tried growing so many different types of things. Some work incredibly well - haskap berries for instance - and some don't work at all - blueberries were a complete fail (we couldn't figure out any way to make those silly plants survive in our yard).

You can either keep trying to make plants that don't really want to grow happy (and expending energy and money into something that just isn't happy in your yard). Or you can give up, keep experimenting and dive headlong in with growing plants you know are thriving right where you're at.

Beautiful spinach that self-seeded in our raised garden bed.

What Should I Grow?

Before you read this chapter, be forewarned it is written from my (ashlee's) extremely practical mindset. I want my yard to produce as much as it possibly can and I want much of that produce to be usable year-round. We have a lot of kids, okay? We need to get as much "free" food as humanly possible.

So, let's separate our produce needs into five groups.

A. Storage Crops
B. Fruit
C. Veggies
D. Herbs
E. Pollinator Plants

Storage crops are one of the most useful things ... ever. If harvested and stored properly, they keep for months. We use a lot of our growing space to grow these types of plants. So, this includes things like potatoes, carrots, beets, rutabagas, squashes and onions among other things.

We are usually able to grow carrots, beets, garlic, potatoes and rutabagas fairly well. But in our case, regular onions are one of those things we just haven't been able to grow well. We have, however, found we can grow chives, leeks and scallions extremely well. So, we grow those things in abundance. I freeze or dry my chives, freeze my leeks and preserve my scallions in salt. I found a simple salt preservation recipe they use in Acadia which I absolutely love (it preserves the scallions for months and preserving them this way makes me feel like an ancient settler which I think is quite fun).

Another good storage crop is drying beans or lentils. Drying beans and lentils keep for years. The plants themselves, however, require a fair amount of growing space. We are experimenting with growing drying beans behind other crops, but have yet to get a harvest more than a small bag full at the end of the year. Because these storage crops are so useful, we are going to keep experimenting and figuring out how to grow them well in a small space.

Fruit is another thing we try to grow as much of as possible. Our goal is to grow enough fruit that we can both eat it fresh and have enough left over to preserve it.

Because we live in a Zone Two area, our immediate thought was that our fruit selection would be extremely limited. But to our surprise, the more research we've done, the more we've found we can grow. We grow grapes, cherries, plums, apples, strawberries, haskaps, raspberries, gooseberries, currants and more. Not all grape varieties grow up here, but we do have some and they are aggressive and hardy growers. The cherries we can grow are small and sometimes a tinch sour, but they are absolutely excellent for preserving ... we've even come to love them fresh. The haskap berries aren't quite as sweet as a blueberry, but our kids eat them so prolifically and with such enthusiasm, you would think haskaps are the sweetest berries of all time. We struggled making raspberries from stores survive, until we were given some from a local farmer and have been absolutely delighted to see them thrive. Our apple tree (and my mom's crabapple tree) produce so abundantly, I struggle to preserve them fast enough (and that is with allowing our kids free reign with the apples - they eat 2-4/day during harvesting season).

We add new varieties and additions to our fruit crop every year and sometimes they don't really work (we have a kiwi vine that just doesn't want to do much of anything) and sometimes we find the fruit isn't that delicious (we've found we don't love goji berries or black currants so we add these berries into mixed jams or smoothies) and sometimes we find we absolutely love this random new fruit (such as ground cherries, solanums and gooseberries).

All this to say, don't think you are unable to grow variety or abundantly in your area. If we live on 0.17 of an acre in an area with wretchedly cold winters and can produce this much, think about what you can do.

This is a picture of our apple tree in bloom and our currant bush to the left. Our yard is SO beautiful and smells so lovely in spring!

Veggies. I LOVE vegetables. If I had not married Josh, there is a high possibility, I would have become a vegetarian - not because I don't like meat, but because I love vegetables more. Our goal with veggies, again, is to have enough to <u>eat fresh and preserve</u>. We grow as many pea plants and beans as we can fit in our space, but our family loves fresh peas and beans so much, we've never produced enough to preserve and that's okay. We grow lettuce in every spot we can think of (one of our daughters loves salad more than dessert so we go through lettuce quite quickly).

And let's look at preserving veggies. Though this is technically a fruit (but everyone thinks of it as a veggie), we grow as many tomatoes as possible. We've found tomatoes to be one of the most versatile things for preserving for winter use. We can them, freeze them, put them in salsa and dehydrate them. They are so useful; I like to have at least ten (if not more) tomato plants growing throughout our yard. Another couple of useful veggies are kale, cabbage and spinach. These veggies can be eaten fresh or frozen or dried for later use. I dry oodles and oodles of kale and then put it in my soups and stews throughout the rest of the year.

In our zone, we've also had trouble growing some veggies. We grow cucumbers (technically a fruit), but have only ever been able to produce enough to eat fresh. So, we buy pounds and pounds of cucumbers from a fruit truck to make pickles. We love peppers (again, technically a fruit), but have only been able to grow a handful of peppers off a plant. It might be our growing season, it might be a need for further knowledge on our part, but we've had trouble with them. So, we rather grow hot peppers (of which we need far fewer) for use in making salsa or pickled hot peppers.

You are able to grow veggies abundantly (even if you live in a small yard), but you may not be able to grow all vegetables abundantly. Figure out what is working in your yard and use your limited space to grow those things. Don't waste valuable real estate on things that just aren't working.

Herbs. Herbs are absolutely one of our favourite things to grow. They require an incredibly little amount of space to grow, usually love it hot (so they're happy in a pot in places all our other plants refuse to grow) and give abundantly throughout the entire year.

Homegrown herbs are in a completely different category than store bought herbs. Their flavour is acutely more potent and the variety you can get is astounding (cinnamon flavoured basil, lemon thyme - the possibilities are nearly endless). Their colour is even different. Look at this dried parsley from my garden (on the left) vs. parsley from the store (on the right). They don't even look like the same thing.

And look at this example. Rosemary from my garden is on the left of the container while rosemary from the store is on the right of the container. Can you see the colour difference? Can you see how much richer and darker my rosemary is?

Because herbs require such a little amount of space, we have them growing in our flower pots, by our grapes (sage helps keep away pests that feed on grapes), in pots on our front deck, in our shade garden beds (parsley and mint grow well in shade!) - you will find herbs here and there and everywhere in our yard.

We harvest the herbs fairly often. Throughout the summer, we cut them back for fresh use (which encourages them to produce even better). And then in the fall, we harvest all of our herbs and dry or freeze them. Between freezing and drying, we usually have enough herbs to last us nearly into the next growing season (and we use our herbs liberally in all of our cooking).

Pollinator Plants. This last group of plants is especially important in your garden. In order for your fruit trees, tomatoes, cucumbers, squashes and so many other plants to flower, be pollinated and then start growing fruit, you need bees and other beneficial insects. The best way to get these beneficial insects into your yard is by planting flowers. So, plant them and plant them everywhere. We have our flowers mixed into our vegetable gardens and pots mixed with herbs and flowers. Because most vegetables and fruits have a hard time growing in shade, we fill the shady parts of our gardens with shade loving flowers.

Doing this works. When we first moved to this location, the yard was a complete disaster. There was overgrown grass and one mostly dead evergreen bush. We brought our tomato plants in pots and were devastated when we only got one or two tomatoes. There simply were no bees around to pollinate those tomato plant flowers.

After five years of adding more and more flowers and fruiting bushes and trees into our yard, our yard is now an absolute hum of insect activity. We often go out in the yard and snap pictures of all sorts of bees buzzing between our flowers and fruit bushes. We've found beetles and worms and ladybugs. We've even started finding bugs we had no idea existed up here.

Birds by the dozens come and go throughout our yard. Where there used to be no bird activity of any sort, we now see dozens washing themselves in our pond and singing in our trees.

37

In the span of a few short years, our yard has been completely revolutionized. It's hard not to get passionate when you see those kinds of changes happening.

Taking the Chickens to Town
{With Jamie Giesbrecht}

When my husband and I first got married, we lived in a small apartment that was lovingly referred to as being "in the ghetto." We grew a few things on the balcony, but were thrilled when we were able to move out of town to our own seven acres. Now, seven acres is not a huge farm, by any means. But it was ours, and we were determined to make use of every square inch. Twelve years later, we have five kids, sheep, bees, horses, mules, goats, pigs - although we have scaled back on this front - geese, ducks, and last but not least, chickens.

One of the first things we did with our property was purchase a chicken-coop-in-a-box, and get a few laying hens — four if I remember correctly — from my mom, who has had a lifetime love of raising chickens. As the years flew by, we noticed changes to city bylaws to allow the keeping of a few hens in backyards for personal use. For some people, and some cities, this has been hotly debated; in other centers, this has been accepted quite simply as a means to be self-sufficient in a world that increasingly requires it.

Food sourcing wasn't on my radar until the last couple of years. Being raised on a small farm myself, I was fairly used to my parents planting a garden, raising chickens and other livestock for sustenance, and plenty of home baking. Lately, it has become more and more popular to be concerned with where our food comes from. "Buy Local" has become a slogan for both supporting local businesses out of ethics (rather than supporting a chain store reaping huge profits) and out of concern for knowing what, exactly, is going into our food. Perhaps equally important is cutting down our environmental impact by ceasing to truck items from far away that we can grow in our own backyards.

People are hugely disconnected from their food sources – this became very clear to me when we started selling eggs from our farm. We had some people not wanting to eat the beautiful blue and green eggs laid by some of our fancy Easter Egger and Olive Egger chickens, simply because the shell wasn't the standard white! Others had spouses or children who wouldn't eat the eggs because they didn't come from the store. All sorts of misperceptions show that we have moved a long ways away from our grandparents' farms and their self-sufficiency.

People had been keeping chickens in the backyards of a small, nearby community for years when a friend in the city decided she had had enough waiting for the bylaws just 20 minutes up the highway to change. If your city doesn't currently allow for the keeping of chickens within the city limits, you can do something about it. Contact your local city hall, and request an audience at a city hall meeting. Be sure to include all the positives of keeping chickens, but don't expect them to allow more than a handful of <u>hens</u> {2-6, depending on the municipality} per family. This is reasonable, and here's why:

> 1. Almost every city bylaw will disallow roosters within the city limits, for good reason. Roosters don't just crow at dawn; they crow all the time. I personally enjoy this sound, but not everyone does.
>
> 2. Chickens do produce waste. Although it can be used in garden beds or composts, most city lots {especially newer, smaller lots in areas of rapid growth} don't have the space to create waste piles for decomposition. It is unlikely a municipality would allow for increased waste in curbside garbage pickups, especially of this nature. A smaller flock ensures a much smaller amount of waste that is easier to manage within the city.
>
> 3. Hens are vocal, too. A respect for the close nature of town living is considerate.
>
> 4. Just like any animal, in greater quantities, there is substantial smell.

<u>Choosing a Breed</u>

Once you have permission to raise backyard chickens, the rest is fun. There are endless numbers of breeds and cross breeds, each with something unique about them. Choosing the best breed for you depends on many things, such as:

1. What color eggs you want. Some chickens, like Easter Eggs, Oliver Eggers, and Copper Marans lay beautiful eggs (blue, olive green, and deep brown, respectively), but it comes at the cost of not laying as many eggs {about 150 eggs in a year, compared to others that may lay up to 300 in a year}.

A range of eggs for, from the left: Goose, Rhode Island Red chicken, Welsh Harlequin duck, Cayuga duck[1], Magpie duck, and Coturnix quail.

---

[1] Just for the sake of interest, I included goose and duck eggs, although they are far too noisy and messy to raise within the city limits. The Cayuga duck lays a beautiful, unique egg with a dark cuticle over it, making the shells look black. When scrubbed it fades – it also fades as the relatively short laying season ends as well.

2. What you want your chicken to look like. Some chickens, such as Frizzles and Polish, look quite exotic, but again, lay considerably less eggs than a more basic bird.

A Frizzle rooster we got from a local fair. Note how puffy he is!

This handsome Frizzle is crossed with a Cochin chicken. He was hatched on our farm, then went to live in town as a house pet for 2 years before returning to our breeding program.

3. If you don't care about looks, and would rather have output, a basic, plain-looking Rhode Island Red or White Leghorn {which

lay a basic brown egg and basic white egg respectively} may lay 200-300 eggs per year.

Once you know what breed you want, you can pursue acquiring it for your backyard in a few different ways.

Buying Hatching Eggs

This is a great way to support a local farmer at a nominal cost. You will have the great joy of watching chicks hatch, but it does require an incubator, and the knowledge of how to run one. Although models are more and more advanced all the time, human error can occur while trying to duplicate nature, ending in a poor hatch {and, I have to say, a heavy heart}. You can also have hatching complications due to poor breeding.

Buying Chicks

Once again, this is a great opportunity to support a local farmer. Prices will vary from inexpensive to quite pricey, depending on the breed. Most farmers sell chicks "straight run", or unsexed, because it is quite hard to sex chicks accurately at a young age {some breeds are auto-sexing, or have certain physical characteristics at birth that make it easy to determine gender; most do not}. This means you will end up with both hens and roosters.

Some people will choose to buy chicks from a reputable hatchery that is experienced in feather-sexing {determining the gender of the chicks based on feather growth patterns} between 1 and 3 days old - although mistakes still happen. Feather sexing can only be done with certain breeds {a rapid feathering breed crossed with a slow feathering breed}, so don't try this at home.

Chicks are the cutest little fluff balls around, but they do require quite a bit of care, no matter if you hatch them yourself, or buy them. On top of shavings as a substrate, fresh water and feed, they require constant heat from a heat lamp at 38 degrees Celsius, reducing by 2 degrees Celsius per week until they are fully feathered OR the use of a radiant heater that can be raised or lowered as the chicks grow. Heat lamps are cheaper to purchase, but can set fires or burn you; radiant heaters need to be raised and lowered as chicks grow but pose absolutely no burn or fire risk.

A key piece of information to keep in mind is that pullets {female chicks} are not mature enough to lay eggs until they are 5-6 months old. Although raising chicks fills me with joy, it might not be your preference. If that is the case, consider buying more mature birds.

Buying Laying Hens

You can purchase older chicks that are closer to maturity from some hatcheries and many farms, but be prepared to pay considerably more. The payoff is that your birds will be ready to lay quite a bit sooner. Some farms may offer mature hens as well - be sure to ask their age, as hens molt {a shedding of feathers for regrowth} after their first full year of laying; production decreases sharply after each molt. Unless you don't mind the lower productivity, stick to younger hens.

Keeping Your Hens

Once you've decided whether to purchase hatching eggs, chicks or fully grown hens, you will need to decide where and how to house them. You can be as creative as you like. You can use something existing or purchase something premade. While farmers in the country have a duty to protect their poultry from foxes, coyotes, and weasels, people in town are not off the hook. Cats will prey on chicks and younger chickens, and might even harass grown hens. Dogs, no matter how well behaved on a leash, may attack and kill chickens with little warning, particularly if they are not accustomed to livestock. Many rural farmers like the idea of free ranging their birds, but this is not an option for an in-town flock, unless your entire yard is fenced, and you can protect your birds from neighboring pets.

Chickens are very hearty through the winter, provided they have shelter from the wind, and can do well in almost all climates. Like any other animal, they rely on fresh water, feed, and shelter. Because keeping fresh water available is an issue in cold temperatures, many people will choose to run a heat lamp or have an insulated shelter where the chickens can run in, and where water has a fighting chance of staying thawed {although a heated dog water bowl that plugs in is also a good option}. Chickens should have good ventilation if kept in a structure, and really do enjoy and appreciate an outside run {which can be enclosed with chicken wire for their protection}. Chickens prefer to sleep up off the ground, and greatly appreciate a ladder-type structure to roost on, as well as some nesting boxes to lay eggs in.

Here are some ideas that some people have used:

A garden shed

- Partition off one side of the shed {so you can still use one side of it for storage} and have the other side for chickens. You can even have a "chicken door" leading to an outdoor run. Since chickens like to sleep up off the ground by instinct {they are easy prey, since they lack the ability to fly well}, consider providing a roost, or a place to perch together. A ladder, a pallet with some of the wood strapping removed, or even a few 2x4's nailed across one end of their indoor section serve well as a roost. Nesting boxes can be purchased {plastic or wood, mountable} or made out of an old bookshelf, dresser, you name it.

Rhode Island red hens perch on either side of a rooster, on a roosting bar.

A chicken-coop-in-a-box.

- This option is very popular, although not cheap. The product is ready to go with no need for independent planning, although most times, they do require assembly. They usually feature nest boxes that can be accessed from outside

48

the structure, a ramp leading up to the nest boxes from the bottom open area, and lots of access doors. They are particularly cute - some models look like barns, or even fancy little houses - but may be expensive or not made exceptionally well.

Our first coop, a boxed model, on our farm in 2010. These are particularly handy for in town.

Providing access to dirt, no matter what your setup, allows the hens to give themselves dust baths. This is not only a part of their natural instinct, but it may also prevent mites.

Feeding Your Hens

Now that your chickens have a home, it's time to choose a feed. While many people like the idea of feeding primarily kitchen scraps, chickens actually do require a certain protein content in order to lay eggs well. My son enthusiastically pursued a science fair project on feeding livestock primarily off of kitchen scraps, but was not able to get ethics approval after the vet consultation due to the inconsistency of nutrient levels in kitchen scraps. Chickens absolutely love scraps, so don't hesitate to provide them, but follow these guidelines to ensure appropriate nutrients in their diet:

1. Feed fresh scraps. Avoid feeding moldy or rotten scraps.
2. Chickens love the parts we throw away from carrots and peppers, but don't enjoy banana peels, or potato skins.
3. Some people feel that pumpkin seeds are a natural dewormer for chickens ~ chickens appreciate Halloween jack-o-lanterns after the holiday. It is a favorite!
4. Avoid feeding processed scraps, such as cooked, buttered, or salted fruit and vegetables. Try to aim for fresh – for example, anything that you cut off, like stalks, leaves, and cores.
5. Avoid feeding meat and dairy, although chickens enjoy bread.

To supplement your scraps, you can:

- choose to mix your own feed, which requires knowing what exactly each grain brings to the mix. You will also have to add in grit which is required by poultry stomachs to grind their food, and oyster shell, required to make the actual egg shell. Otherwise, you will have soft eggs that are covered in nothing but a thick, see-through membrane.
- purchase a commercial feed or
- buy from a local farmer.

I have tried all three methods, and my preference is to buy a balanced commercial feed that contains actual, recognizable seeds as opposed to a commercial pellet feed. The pellet feeds are more highly processed and produce a much more foul-smelling waste. Commercial feeds are labelled in such a manner that it is easy to tell which one to buy for which stage of bird {chick starter, medicated and non-medicated - and the medicated part is a personal preference - chick grower, and layer ration, for example}.

If you choose to purchase feed ration from a local farmer, be aware that it might not be a complete feed. Often, an ingredient, such as oyster shells, must still be added.

Quail

Quail are a much smaller bird than a chicken and are very easily raised in town {where permitted}. I know someone raising dozens of them in his city garden {protected from predators}. They do have a trilling call, but it is fairly quiet. Quail can start laying eggs at the early age of just 6 weeks old, making them very appealing for those who want produce sooner. The eggs are small, though, just a little bigger than your thumb nail and are rich with an almost buttery taste. Quail lay eggs well, are hearty, and can be eaten as a small meat bird. They are a delicacy in some places.

Coturnix quail eggs, which can be mottled brown to light blue in color.

Final Touches

I relish my moments in the coop when I go out to collect the eggs – eggs I use to bake fresh goods for my 5 children and my husband. There is nothing more satisfying! To make the most out of your chicken-rearing experience, and to make your town flock comfortable, try the following:

1. Add shavings to the nesting areas, and on any floor surface of the indoor portion of the shelter. Straw, once wet with waste, sticks together and hardens into large masses that can be heavy and hard to remove. I prefer not to use straw for this reason.
2. Either hang a chicken feeder, which prevents hens scratching at the feed and wasting it, or make simple feeder of your own {please note, there are special feeders for chicks}
3. Purchase a chicken waterer that holds enough water to last a few days, or use something on hand {please note: to prevent drowning, use a proper chick watering device for young birds}.
4. Hang a head of lettuce or cabbage from the shelter structure of your coop, and watch the birds peck and enjoy this special treat!

All that is left to do is put your birds in their new home, secure all the hatches, and wait for those first backyard eggs! Enjoy.

Bringing the Bees to Town
{With Jamie Giesbrecht}

Scaping honey from a frame in early fall.

As more and more people - and municipalities - realize the importance of food security and the benefit of allowing people to produce food in their own backyards, changes to bylaws are taking place. Some municipalities now allow for small scale beekeeping within the city limits. Because this is new on many fronts, your first step is to approach your local city bylaw enforcement, and inquire as to the availability in your area.

Reasons for Beekeeping

I'm an advocate for beekeeping for many reasons:

1. Contrary to popular belief, bees rarely sting. They can, of course, if threatened. To put things in perspective, though, my husband harvested our honey frames last year without a bee suit, and was not stung at all {he did use a moderate amount of smoke to calm the bees, but it was one of his best experiences so far}. We cannot confuse wasps and bees - their behavior is quite different. We have 2 hives directly behind our house and have experienced no increase in insect stings in our very active, outdoors-loving children. Bee stings are not a reason to disallow beekeeping in municipalities {although we should be sensitive to those with allergies}.
2. Our world bee population is in trouble. We need MORE people to raise bees!
3. Honey can be substituted in many recipes, rather than using the standard white sugar {which is processed to be made white - if you're seeking to consume whole foods, home-raised honey is a great option}. I use our family-produced honey in tea, home-made bread, and other baking rather than purchasing the traditional white sugar. If you can raise bees, you are raising your own baking ingredients.

Getting Set Up

There are more items required to raise backyard bees than backyard chickens. Most of the components are highly specialized, and not easily duplicated at home for a beginner. Don't let that phase you. Here's what you need to look for:

1. Find a bee supplier. For a first time beekeeper, I recommend purchasing a 'started' bee colony with a queen the workers are already attached to. These bee colonies are usually started on a cardboard frame in a specialized cardboard box that is easy to insert into your own {empty} hive.
2. Set up a basic hive, which includes:
    a. **a base** {this has openings for the worker bees to come and go}
    b. **a foundation with frames** {this is where the bees will start to collect honey, and where they will eat from in winter - DO NOT collect honey from this portion}
    c. **a queen excluder** {this allows worker bees to pass to the upper honey supers - the part you will collect honey from for your consumption - but doesn't allow the queen through. She shouldn't travel up into the collection frames. Without the queen, the whole hive is lost!}
    d. **honey super with frames** {once the lower frames in the foundation are full, worker bees fill the honey super frames - these are the

frames we remove and collect our honey from}
   e. **the lid** {which allows access for worker bees to come and go}.
3. Hives usually come in plain, unpainted wood, although you may find some prefinished. If you would like to paint your hive to help it withstand the weather, use a water-based paint. Paint fumes can be bothersome to bees.
4. Assemble and place your hive at the back of your yard. Bees will travel up to 3.5 kilometers {and some sources say much further!} to pollinate, so you do not need to worry about positioning it close to gardens or flowers. Bees stay in the hive overnight. During the day, if your hive is thriving, you will be able to see bees zipping in and out, and hear a pleasant buzz.
5. Don't plan to harvest honey until the fall season, so that the bees have as long as possible to collect.
6. Obtain a bee suit, if you wish, although my husband is going without these days. I advise the use of a smoker - although honey bees are docile, it is more pleasant for them, and less anxiety-inducing for you, to use a smoker. The smoker will put the bees into conservation mode, and they will retreat to the bottom of the hive.
7. Bees don't require food over the winter if you have allowed them to collect and keep a reserve in the foundation frames. If not, you will need to feed them a sugar syrup. I do recommend allowing them to

collect and feed off their own supply, as they would in nature.

Harvesting Your Honey

This is definitely the best part! All that waiting is well worth it. Here's what to do:

1. Don your bee suit, if you plan to wear one, and prep your smoker.
2. As you open the lid, use your smoker to put the bees in a conservation mode. If ants or wasps have taken over the hive, which can happen in a year of drought, you will notice very little honey on your frames. This is extremely disappointing.
3. Remove the honey super frames, and close the lid.
4. The frame should be thick with waxy honeycombs just oozing with honey. Placing the frame over a large, clean container, you can use a spatula, flipper, or other flat tool to scrape the honeycombs, wax and all, off.

5. You will notice some blemishes in the honey, and possibly even the odd perished worker bee. Not to worry. Place a sieve {you can use a jam or jelly sieve, but our favorite is a pot lid sieve that sits over a large cooking pot}, over another clean container, and scoop moderate amounts onto or into the sieve. Plan to allow the honey to drip through at its own pace, which is slow. This will separate out and remove wax and impurities.
6. We do not process or pasteurize our honey any further. We spoon the strained honey directly into glass canning jars, usually the 250mL size for convenience, and store in the cupboard.

<u>Enjoy!</u>

Home-raised honey has a delightful taste to it. Typically, it is lighter in color than the store bought variety, and is much easier to wipe up. It doesn't seem as sticky, and I would consider it thinner. Home-raised honey can vary in flavor, depending on what crops or flowers the bees have been accessing. I haven't yet found a variety I don't like! This natural sweetener is a gift to your family, every day.

Now, back to Josh and Ashlee - it's time to take a look at your yard!

Making Your Yard Work for You

We hope we've planted a spark. We hope you realize how capable you and your yard are of producing abundantly. But maybe you've reached this point and you're a bit lost. You want to start implementing these new growing ideas and chickens and bees but you don't know where to start.

Do you want raised garden beds or do you want to plant right in the dirt? Do you want your fruit trees all in one section or scattered throughout the yard? Where do you put that chicken coop and run?

In this chapter, we'll go through pros and cons of different yard styles and also give you a couple sample plans to hopefully help get you started in your own food producing journey.

In our own yard, we have both raised beds and ground level beds. Both have positives and negatives.

<u>Raised Bed Positives</u>

1. Fewer weeds
2. You can control your soil content fairly adequately (you know what you are putting in there)
3. Easier on the back for weeding, harvesting, etc.
4. Thaws earlier in the spring and can be planted sooner
5. Potentially takes up less space than ground level beds

Raised Bed Negatives

1. Requires financial investment[2]
2. Hard to deal with the plants in the middle of the raised bed
3. The soil settles and needs to be topped up nearly every year

Ground Level Bed Positives

1. Requires no investment
2. Can grow plants in rows and walk between rows
3. Quick to prepare and get plants in the ground

Ground Level Bed Negatives

1. Soil will most likely need to be amended to grow things well
2. If the bed is close to the grass, you will often have grass growing into the bed
3. Weeds are more prolific than in a raised bed

---

[2] You need to buy lumber and growing medium for your raised beds. We tried making our raised beds from old pallets because we simply didn't have the funds at the time. Working with the pallets was extremely aggravating and left us with a bed which buckled over time. We have had to add extra lumber for support, which has dealt with the buckling, but it is not pretty. It is a useful, but not beautiful space.

On to the next question, should you grow your fruit trees all together or spread out throughout your yard. In our yard, we have our trees spread throughout. We like this as it puts points of interest all over our yard, however, we have found some negatives. As the trees are getting bigger, they are casting more and more shade around them. This changes the growing conditions of the beds the trees happen to be in. Beds that were once nearly full sun are now partial sun which means we simply can't grow as many vegetables in those beds.

If we were to start our yard from scratch again, we would most likely plant our trees together, like in an orchard, and have fruit bushes throughout the yard for interest. But ... maybe not. It is SO nice having trees scattered throughout the yard. It makes our yard feel more woodsy and less open to the public eye. It is a hard toss up.

When thinking about where to put your chicken coop or beehives, be sure to look into your municipality's bylaws. Where we live all structures need to be a minimum of six feet from the property line. With that in mind, we scratched our original idea of where to place our chicken coop. We ended up putting it fairly close to our backdoor (so it is a quick run back and forth in winter), close to electricity (so we could run an electric cord over for a heat lamp) and with a good amount of sunlight so those chickens can go bask in the sun on warm days.

Here's a picture of our chicken coop. Josh also added a play fort on top to make it dual purpose (which the kids are incredibly grateful for).

Want a little more inspiration and direction? Here are some plans Josh and I put together to get you thinking.

Plan # 1
The actual dimensions of the plan

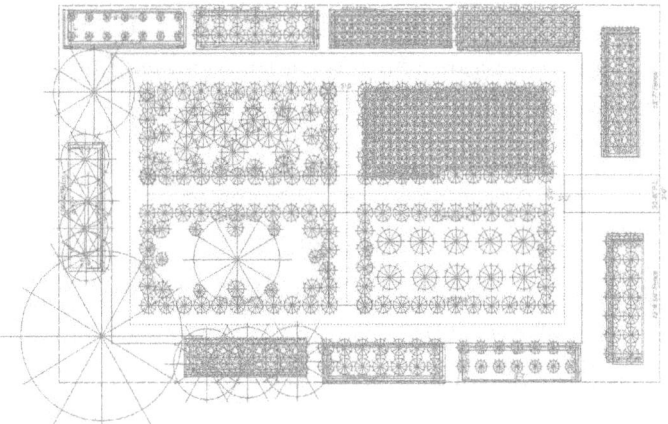

The design in plain sight

If you can believe it, this plan is structured for a small yard. With a meagre growing space of 50' x 30' you can fit in this many veggies and fruits. If you have a larger yard, you can easily subdivide one section of the yard to allow this type of planting and still have plenty of outdoor space for entertaining, toys, chickens, bees, etc.

Along the fence line, you can plant fruit bearing bushes (as many as space will allow (read up on the plant to figure out what mature height and width it will be)) and even put a fruit bearing tree in the corner. Also think of vertical space, things like grapes, cucumbers, squashes and tomatoes can easily be trained up a fence while things like strawberries and herbs can grow in small containers attached onto the fence (we've seen eavestrough, old boots and wooden pallets used as the containers!).

Have small garden beds with paths between to allow easy access to the entire space for planting, weeding and harvesting. The paths allow you to walk around, examine and care for your plants without damaging any other plants by stepping on them. It seems simple, but it is an easy thing to forget.

If you have back issues, consider doing a design like this, but having all the beds raised. At a higher height, you can sit on a stool and weed, plant or harvest.

Also think about having a concrete, brick or gravel path (with landscape fabric beneath) between your garden beds. If your beds are at ground level, having a path like this will eliminate most grass from getting into your bed (some grass and weeds will probably still find a way to your bed because they are crazy like that, but it won't be nearly as much).

Plan # 2 - The Rough Sketch

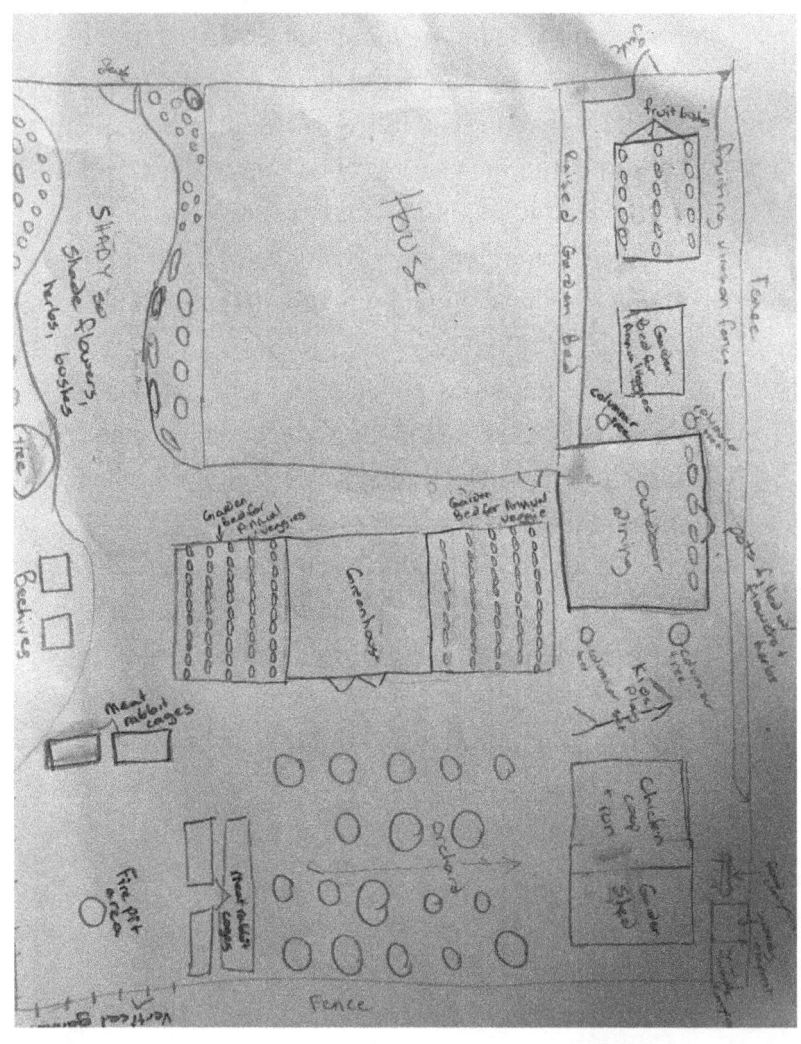

This is how I (ashlee) do up garden plans. I let my imagination go crazy and sketch in all my ideas. After I have a general idea of where I want things and know approximately how big the space is,

I go back and get actual dimensions of plants, the structures and space. I also look through in more detail the soil and sun requirements for the plants I want. The main point of this drawing is to get all your ideas out and figure out how you want the yard to flow. After you have this plan, you can come back and tweek and adjust it to suit your needs and your yard's characteristics.

As we mentioned previously, in our yard, the gardens, trees and bushes are spaced throughout. We see our yard as being one giant edible piece of land with just enough space for fun and outdoor living. Because our front yard is accessible by deer, we have filled the front space with flowers, pretty bushes, a few edibles here and there (because we always start a trillion things and we always run out of spots to put them), a small pond, a bird feeder and a few raised pots with edibles.

Everything behind the fence is up for garden beds and edibles. When you first come through the gate, we have our "apple tree bed." The apple tree bed has become quite shady as the tree has grown so we have currants in the sunny corners and whatever will grow under the apple tree (a few strawberries plants and quite a few flowers are seeming quite happy).

To the right of this bed and across the grass is one of our garden beds - this one gets a lot of sun and is one of our best growers. In the corners of this bed we have a goji berry and a gooseberry (as well as a row of tulips ... just because they make us happy).

Going down along our house, the space is fairly narrow and shady in spots. Along the house, we have shade loving flowers and ferns and shade tolerating herbs (like mint and parsley). We also put in a huckleberry and are waiting to see if it will produce anything. Two of our honeyberry bushes are along this often-shady stretch of house - I wasn't expecting them to do too much in that spot, but they are thriving. On the other side of this fairly narrow space is our fence. Along this sunny fence line, we have a small bed with wild flowers and then another bed with our raspberries, strawberries, more honeyberries and solanums.

Part of the shade bed along our house.

After coming out from alongside the house, you come into our "real" backyard. In this part of our yard, you will find our chicken coop and play fort, a raised garden bed along the fence (we grow lots of annual veggies, but we also have rhubarb and chives that come back every year in there), a plum tree and shade plant bed, a cherry tree bed, small garden boxes for each of our children, a crabapple tree, our storage shed, Josh's shop, our deck and greenhouse and a fire pit/entertaining space.

Part of our L shaped raised garden bed that goes along the fence.

Going to the right side of our house, we have three more garden beds (one being a rock garden bed which has helped us grow some sun loving veggies a bit better than normal), a grape, a pear tree, an apricot tree and a sandpit/pool area.

And all that in a 0.17-acre yard.

We seriously love our yard so much. From spring to fall, there is ALWAYS something blooming or ready to harvest. And even though it takes a fair amount of work to upkeep, it is the most rewarding way to spend time.

I have sometimes heard people say they want to make their yard more "kid friendly." So, they get rid of garden beds and add more toys or something like that. Our yard has spots to entertain our kids, but its main priority is to feed our family. And even though this is our yard's priority, our kids are outside most of the day from the first signs of spring until the late fall. They dig in their sandpit, play in their fort, watch the chickens, pick flowers and find things to eat. They colour on rocks and pretend to be spies. The yard has never been geared towards children, but they l.o.v.e. it out there. You can have a space that is useful and the best of the best playgrounds for children.

Supplementing Your Yard

Foraging, Hunting and Fishing

{With Josh and Ashlee Kirschner and Jamie Giesbrecht}

** Before we start this chapter, it is important we state this is not a guide on how to hunt or forage. We simply want to get you thinking. Foraging for berries and weeds can be extremely productive, but you need to be careful and take time to study. Some berries and weeds are poisonous and can make you violently ill or even kill you. We don't say this to scare you, but to caution you. Take time to study foraging books well before you start on this journey. **

Nothing gets you in touch with nature like hunting and foraging. When you forage, you find plants in their natural environment. You learn to look for signs of them - you smell them out, you find areas you know they would love. You become an expert in your habitat.

The more you study foraging, the more you realize nature has already given you most everything you need to survive. Things like wild strawberries, high bush cranberries, saskatoons and mint grow prolifically and are ready for you to use if you simply took the time to find them. Spruce tips and bark can be used. The more and more you research, the more you find so much of the forest around you is edible.

    For a long time, Josh tried to convince me (ashlee) that we needed to start foraging and harvesting from the land around us. I kept shrugging the idea off, thinking "Don't you know how busy I am?" Until one day, I finally gave in and we went looking for berries with Josh's treasured "Boreal Herbal Book." I was absolutely astounded. As we perused the book and walked farther down the hiking trail, the more and more things I saw we could eat. Some berries were sour, but being a cook, I immediately had ideas of what they would taste good in.

    I came home and thought for quite a while. And I was surprised to realize that I was convicted. I was convicted that I wanted the ease of the grocery store so much that I didn't take the time to harvest the overwhelming abundance around me. I was exalting ease over making good use of what was already right in front of me. I realized how wasteful and selfish I was being.

    Yes, knowing how to forage well requires a fair amount of knowledge. Foraging is a skill - it takes time to learn the signs of where the food is and knowing when it's ready and to know which thing is which. But I realized taking the time to learn that skill would only lead to benefit in my life.

    The more I know, the more confident I become. When we go hiking, the fear of getting lost is lessened because I know we can find foods we could eat to survive. And when I make preserves with things our family picked from the woods. Oh man. I feel SO proud of what we've done (and it tastes out of this world which is an added bonus).

Fireweed, wild raspberries, strawberries and highbush cranberries.

But let's stop for a moment and think about things right in your hometown. "What?!" you say. "There are things in my hometown I could eat?" Yes, there are.

The weeds in your own garden.[3] Those super plants that pop up nearly everywhere in your garden. So many of those are completely edible and can become part of your diet. Dandelions tops and roots are completely edible. We fry up lamb's quarters (a weed) in butter and it is absolutely divine. So much of what we see as problem plants are actually completely edible and ready to use.

And be on the lookout for other things in your community. In our town, people often let their crabapples, apples and chokecherries just fall to the ground. So many people can't even be bothered to harvest and eat what is growing in their own yards! Be on the lookout and ask those people if they would mind you harvesting their fruit in exchange for a few jars of preserves made from their

---

[3] We highly recommend ONLY eating weeds from your own garden. You never know what kind of chemicals have been sprayed in public parks or your neighbour's yards.

produce. They would probably say yes (even without the preserves) because you're saving them from cleaning a big mess in the late fall.

Hunting and fishing are other ways to make use of the land around you. Although hunting requires a large financial investment at the beginning (as well as time learning and getting licenses), it is extremely beneficial. When you hunt, you harvest animals that have been eating organically. You know, for the most part, what their diet would have been and it far surpasses what you can find in the supermarket. Besides that, when you get a large animal, such as a moose, you are providing your family with meat for a season, not simply a few days. Hunting connects you directly with the food you eat.

Fishing, like hunting, is another great way to harvest from the land around you. Fishing requires a much smaller financial investment than hunting, but is also incredibly beneficial. In exchange for spending time on the beach or in a boat, you can take home fish to fill your freezer and feed your family. And the health benefits of fish are quite astounding - from helping your heart and brain to contributing to overall good health. It is one of the healthiest foods you will ever eat.

Now that you're eager and ready to go hunting and fishing, we should do a quick run through of what you need to know before you start. As a fore note, this is not legally binding information. We are simply sharing what we have found as we've implemented hunting and fishing into our lifestyle.

1. Before you can start hunting, in British Columbia, Canada (rules may differ in your area), you need to take a few courses. The first is the C.O.R.E which stands for Conservation and Outdoor Recreation Education. After you've taken that course, you can acquire a hunter number or Fish and Wildlife I.D. This number allows you to legally hunt and fish in British Columbia.

2. If you want to hunt with a rifle, you need to take another course. In British Columbia, that course is called P.A.L which stands for Possession and Acquisition License. Getting this license allows you to buy ammunition and non-restricted firearms.

3. After you have gone through the courses and gotten your ammunition and firearm, you need to purchase tags for each individual large game animal you want to hunt. So, if you want to hunt for both moose and deer, you need to buy two tags (one for the moose and one for the deer). Again, remember all of this information is based on what we know living in British Columbia.

4. You can only hunt for certain animals at certain times of the year. Hunting season for most large game animals is only open in the fall months.

5. If you want to fish, you also have to get a license, but the paperwork is not as detailed as hunting. In British Columbia, you need to have a Fish and Wildlife I.D. number and then you can purchase your fishing license.

To see more government information on hunting and fishing in your area, refer to a website like this.

https://www2.gov.bc.ca/gov/content/sports-culture/recreation/fishing-hunting/hunting/regulations-synopsis

So now you have all the paperwork ready, and you're ready to hunt or fish. Now you face the where, the how and the wait.

Where Can You Go Hunting or Fishing?[4]

1. You can go hunting on private land, but only with written permission from the landowner.
2. You can also hunt on crown land.

How Is This Going to Work?

Before you start hunting, you need to know how to do a few things. And think a bit ahead as well.

---

[4] Hunting and fishing regulations will also show you where you can and cannot go hunting and fishing. You can also easily find information on government websites about this.

1. Obviously, you need to know how to use your rifle. It needs to be sighted in and ready to go before you even hit the trail to go hunting.
2. You need to know how to field dress an animal
3. You need to think about how you will get the animal or fish back to your base and then how you will get the animal back home or to a local butcher's. (Do you have game bags, garbage bags, etc. for transport?)
4. Then wait. Be prepared that you might get skunked. Hunters and fishers sometimes go weeks, months, even years without getting any meat. This is a reality - sometimes you can know a lot and hunt at the right time in the right place, and the animals will still stay away.

And now you're at the last part. You can either hire a butcher to package the meat up for you or learn to do it yourself.

That's it! You can now bring home a freezer full of meat.

Helpful Note - We HIGHLY recommend you go out hunting with a seasoned hunter. The very best way to learn is to shadow someone who has been doing this for a long time - they know the tricks and things to watch for.

Recipes for Your Foraged Items
{from Jamie Giesbrecht}

Now that you have collected a wide variety of berries through foraging, it is time to put them to use! Here are a few suggestions:

- **Rustic Pastry Dough**
    - This dough can be used for small, handheld pies, large, sheet-pan pies {did you know you can make a rectangular pie in a cookie sheet?}, as a casserole topper, or as a traditional pie crust. You can expect to make 3 traditional pies with this recipe, 1 slab pie or sheet pan pie, and about 4-5 pies with minimal, decorative toppers.
    - Mix together 4 cups of flour, 1 tsp of salt, 1 tbsp of sugar, and 1 tsp of baking powder. Using a pastry blender {a fork will do if you don't have one}, 'cut' in 1 ¾ cups of shortening and blend until you have a crumbly dough. Add 1 egg, ½ cup of cold water, and 1 tbsp of vinegar. Mix just enough to combine {try not to over mix}. You can chill the dough to make it extra flakey, or use it right away if you don't have time. Roll out on a floured surface; use as desired on almost anything!

- **Top-Up Pie**
    - This versatile pie is simple. Once you've made your favorite pie crust, core and slice a

few apples - maybe 4 tart apples, preferably crab apples or apples you've grown in your yard {don't be afraid to ask neighbors that don't use their apples if you can pick them - one year, we received 3 industrial garbage cans full of apples that would otherwise have been let to fall to the ground and rot, because people didn't want to use them or didn't know how} .

Picking the bounty from someone who didn't plan to use their apples.

- Shake a couple of tablespoons of flour onto the apples. Add ½ - ¾ cup of brown sugar {for a delicious, caramel taste}.
- Sprinkle with about 1 tsp of cinnamon, and a ¼ - ½ tsp of nutmeg.
- Add 1 - 2 cups of foraged berries, such as raspberries, wild strawberries, saskatoons, or wild blueberry.

- Use some leftover pie dough and some cookie cutters to make a unique pie topper.
- Bake at 350C until the top is nicely browned {45 minutes to an hour}

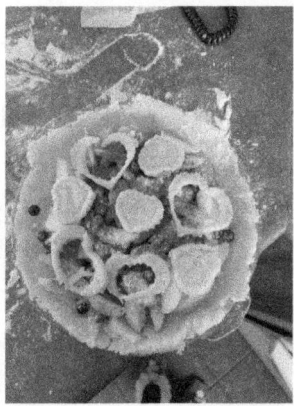

A peach-apple-saskatoon pie. Anything goes with a top-up pie

Mini pies are adorable and an amazing treat in a lunchbox!

Foraged Jam

- Pectin is a thickener used to help make jellies and jams 'gel", so they aren't too runny. Pectin boxes and canning books commonly list sugar content and canning times required for jams. However, you won't likely find a recipe listed for saskatoon jam or wild strawberry jam, or a combination of your favorite, wild berries. Find the closest berry you can, and go for it! For saskatoon jam, use the blueberry recommendations {for sugar content and canning time} found on the recipe list inside your pectin box. Likewise, for wild strawberries, use the strawberry guidelines. If you plan to mix everything together to make what I call a jumble-jam, choose one main ingredient berry - a berry with the highest concentration in your jam. For example, if the jam is predominantly saskatoon berries, followed by raspberries and a few wild strawberries, follow the blueberry guidelines.
- Rosehip jelly is a favorite of mine, back from my days of living in Yukon, Canada. A tip from my mom for making this jelly the best it can be is to wait until after the first frost before picking the berries. The berries will darken after frost, and soften. The flavor

comes through in a whole new way, making it worth the wait!

- **Anything Muffins**
    - Take a basic blueberry muffin recipe, and substitute fresh or frozen berries you have foraged for the store-bought suggestion.
    - Add a teaspoon of cinnamon to the batter, and ¼ tsp of nutmeg, if you'd like.
    - Consider using a multigrain flour to make an even healthier treat {I prefer this over even whole wheat flour} - I usually use 1 cup of white flour to every 1 cup of multigrain flour so the recipe is not too heavy.
    - You can experiment with using honey as a sweetener instead of sugar. As another option, consider brown sugar, which is less processed than white sugar.
    - You can substitute goat's milk from your own goats at the same volumes as cow's milk from the store.
    - You may choose to top the muffins with a sprinkle of brown sugar before baking.

Some freshly picked saskatoons, ready to be used in the kitchen.

Foraged Tea

A few years ago, I had the privilege of attending 'Kema' at Doig River First Nations reserve. Kema is a place of happiness; it is being in the bush, surrounded by water or nature. It was an amazing experience to bring about personal peace and awareness. We went with the elders who have incredible knowledge of the land. One of my favorite parts was learning about making tea. It was the first time I had ever considered making my own tea, let alone using foraged goods to do so. Now my kids enjoy picking berries just for this purpose. What kind and what combinations are totally up to you, and your tastes. You can even include pine needles, which provide a strong taste - some people feel pine needles hold some healing qualities as well.

Once you have picked a variety of items, dry them on a cookie sheet {or refer to the section of this book on drying for alternate ideas}. That's it! This simple tea can be enjoyed by adding the dry components directly to boiling water as we did at Kema. Your lips act as a natural filter, although some people choose to consume the tea ingredients as well; you can also use a mesh tea infuser. For this method, loosely pack your dried ingredients in the mesh basket or ball infuser, and allow it to soak in boiling water, adding milk and honey to your taste.

Josh and I also make our own tea mix as well. We use foraged mint or some from our yard, wild chamomile (we have found it in our driveway), lemon balm, dried apples (even dried apple skins) from our tree and fireweed flowers. With a bit of local honey, it is absolutely delicious (and it looks pretty too!).

Making Your Abundance Last

You've worked hard all summer. You've babied seeds, watered plants, weeded garden beds, gone foraging and suddenly without realizing it, you have piles and piles of produce on your kitchen table, in your mudroom and quite literally all over your house. There is no way you can eat all this food before it goes bad. So what are you going to do?

Preserve!!! You're going to preserve it, right, right? I'll answer for you. "Yes, that's right, Mrs. Kirschner, we're going to preserve it and make sure it doesn't get wasted."

I'm so happy to hear that - so proud of you for making that decision. Now, that you've decided to preserve, let's have a quick look at some of the different preserving options.

You can

1. Dry
2. Can
3. Pressure Can
4. Freeze

Drying

Difficulty Level: Easy

The first option, we'll go through in a bit more detail is drying. Drying is one of my favourite options. It is SO simple. I have two dehydrators (see the picture below) which I use regularly throughout harvest season. I dry things like herbs, tomatoes (when I have enough - I use tomatoes for so many other things, I don't always have enough to do this!), apples and kale.

But you don't have to have a dehydrator to dry things. You can tie your herbs together with burlap string and then hang them upside down in your pantry or really any place where they will get some air flow.

Or you can make a contraption like this (see the picture below). If you want to make your own, the most important thing is making sure there is air flow. Once you have something like this, it is easy to sun dry tomatoes or really anything!

Also, quick note before moving on from this. I have discovered I can make my own fruit leather with my dehydrator! How cool is that?

My jars of dried herbs

Dried Purple Kale - it is one of the prettiest things on my shelf.

Canning

Difficulty Level: Medium

When I first started canning (the first thing I canned was applesauce I think), I was terrified. I was terrified about germs and botulism (aka food poisoning) and accidentally killing Josh with those horrible germs. After talking with my mentor, she laughed and said, "Ashlee, you will be fine." (I cannot even count how many times people have told me that - I must be over dramatic or something).

But let's be honest for a minute. There is risk of botulism whenever you can something; that's just a fact. You need to preserve things properly and up to code, but that doesn't mean you need to be terrified. You can learn to do this and do it well!

Here's what you need to do to get started. (And this is not a comprehensive guide or anything like that - this is me sharing what I've learned. I hope it helps!)

1. Buy your equipment. You'll need a water bath canner and a jar rack (some people don't use the jar rack, but I find it super handy and wouldn't can without it).

2. Buy your jars. You have to get mason jars to can! It will make more sense later, so keep reading.
3. Buy the proper sized snap lids for your mason jars. Snap lids are basically lid inserts for the top of your mason jars - just google it, it's not scary or complicated. There are three sizes of snap lids (small, medium and large), but the most common are by far small or large these days.

   For your reference, here's a picture of the jar, band and lid insert.

Now that you have your equipment, you need to decide what you want to can. When deciding what to can or which recipe to use, it is important to find a recipe either approved by the USDA (or some other food governing source you can rely on and trust) or one that follows the canning guidelines set out on the USDA food preservation website. Again, we need to be aware there is a risk of botulism so don't just make up your own recipe and can it. Be safe!

You can water bath-can fruit (like canned peaches, applesauce, etc.), jams, jellies, salsa and pickled vegetables. All of these things have a high acidity content and are hence safe to water bath can (just make sure you use a good recipe!).

Once your produce is ready to go, you need to prepare your jars and canner. This part was a little daunting to me at first, but it's really no big deal!

In order to prepare your jars, you need to sterilize them. I sterilize my jars by putting them in the sink and pouring boiling water over them. While you're waiting for the water to boil, fill your canner with water and get it heating on the stove.

I do sterilize the jars and the outer bands with boiling water, but I do not sterilize snap lids. I read in one of my canning books (a popular one, but I can't remember which right now) it is better to wash these in hot soapy water. If you look closely at your snap lid insert, you will see there is something like rubber around the edge. This rubber will basically melt onto the top of your mason jar hence sealing and protecting it from going rancid. If you put boiling water on it, it is possible that the rubber seal will be compromised.

Once your jars are ready, fill them up with your precious preserves (be sure the preserves are still hot). Make sure the top of the jar is clean (remember that the lid insert "rubber" basically has to melt on to the top of the jar to seal - so make sure there is nothing (even water droplets) preventing that from happening). Once clean, place the snap insert on and twist the outer band on (make sure the band is firm, but not too tight). Finally, gently place your jars in your canner that should be at this point at a rapid boil. Keep them in the canner at a full boil for however long your recipe requires.

Take your jars out and wait to hear that blessed popping noise. Once you hear that (and see it with an indention - again google it), you know it is sealed and safe to store.

A few notes to mention.

- Sometimes jars have a false seal. So, they look like they have sealed, but they really haven't. That happens to us every once in a while, and it is really annoying (and has brought me to tears at times). One of my friends stores her jars with the bands off so it is easy to tell if this has happened. Just be aware this can happen sometimes. If this does happen, you need to throw out whatever was in that jar. You no longer know if it is safe to eat or not.

- You can only use your snap lid inserts ONCE. After they have been used once, their integrity and ability to seal well is gone.

- Make sure you work fairly quickly when putting things in your jar and then into the canner. You need to make sure the temperature differences aren't drastic between your preserves, your jars and the water in the canner. I've had a jar of peaches explode in my canner - it wasn't dangerous, but it did make me terribly upset - and we think the issue was a difference in temperature.

- There are different issues you might have as you start canning (jar exploding like me, something just not sealing, etc.). There are so many resources on the internet or books in your library to help if you have any issues. Don't lose heart - there is an answer for your canning woes!

Pressure Canning

Difficulty Level: Medium-Difficult

Why on earth would you pressure can? What even is a pressure canner? Good questions.

If you read the last note on canning, you would have noticed I wrote you are able to water bath can anything with a high enough acidity level (so fruits, pickled veggies, etc.), but what about things that aren't acidic enough? What if you want to preserve your beans and you don't want to pickle them?

That's where a pressure canner comes in. It cans things at a higher temperature and pressure (hence being called a pressure canner) than a water bath canner and hence allows you to safely preserve things that aren't highly acidic.

You prepare the jars and produce mostly the same as with a water bath canner, but it gets different after you stick the jars into the pressure canner. The pressure canner lid needs to be secured on, it needs to be brought up to pressure, processed for the required time (timing changes depending on your altitude) and then the pressure canner needs to cool before opening the lid (if you get impatient and open the lid too soon or don't secure the lid properly, the lid can explode off ... in other words this is for the more advanced preserver). This method of preserving is not at all undoable, but it is more complicated. I would suggest getting comfortable with the easier methods of preserving and then move into pressure canning. And maybe even pressure can with a seasoned pro a few times before going out on your own. They are always full of helpful tricks!

If you get a big bunch of beans or what not and don't feel ready to pressure can yet, don't worry. You can pickle, freeze or dry them - you still have options!

Freezing

Difficulty Level - Easy

Freezing is an incredibly easy way to preserve your produce until you're ready to use it. The only downside is there never seems to be enough room in my freezers to keep everything.

In order to freeze your produce, it can be blanched (blanching means putting it into boiling water briefly and then putting it into cold water) or cooked beforehand. It is said blanching helps stop flavour, colour and texture loss when you freeze things ... but I have a confession. I rarely blanch things ... I know, I should be ashamed. But I haven't noticed a difference between things that are blanched and are not blanched so I was having a hard time seeing the point. I do sometimes roast things (like beets) before I freeze them- does that make me a better person?

One thing I've found really handy when freezing produce is to measure and label. So, if I have a bunch of rhubarb I want to freeze, I'll measure out 4 cups and then label, "4 cups Rhubarb, June 1, 2020." Having the date helps me know which bag needs to be used first and knowing the amount is super helpful for using that produce in recipes.

The last thing I should mention in the preserving section is root vegetables (so those vegetables that grow underground like carrots, potatoes, etc.). These don't need to be frozen, dried or canned; they should keep on their own in a cool, dark place for quite a long time.

There are some things to note about this as well. When you harvest potatoes and other root vegetables, you need to get some of the dirt off, but the main concern is making sure they are dry. Any moisture on your root vegetables can lead to them going rotten. So, make good and sure they are dry before you put them in a bin.

Another quick note with potatoes, they MUST be stored in darkness. If you do not store your potatoes in darkness, they will turn green. I didn't think that was much of an issue until I read the green can indicate the presence of toxins that are quite dangerous to humans. Our potatoes started turning green after a few weeks in the greenhouse (yes, I know, it was a bad decision to keep them there, but at the time I had nowhere else to store them). So, all that to say, I have no idea how potatoes can be sold in stores without going green (maybe they add something to them? I really don't know!).

One last thing before I end this chapter, we've found carrots can't be stored exactly the same way as other root vegetables. I have an absolutely wonderful root vegetable bin Josh made me - which I love with all of my heart - and I quickly purchased a huge sack of carrots to store in it. We unfortunately found over time, the carrots started going limp. Which is okay sort of ... but who really wants a limp carrot with dip?

We googled it and found if you keep your carrots in layers in a big bucket (with a lid) in moist wood shavings, they will keep crunchy and well for a long time. Google has helped us so many times - thanks, sweet friend!

This is how we store our carrots - in damp wood shavings in a large bucket. Very simple!

These are pictures of my preserving wall. If you remember from earlier, Josh and I live in a 900 sq. ft house with 4 children. My canning obsession was starting to take over our entire kitchen so we strategized and Josh built me these wonderful shelves. The shelves hold about 70 large jars of canning (more than that if I use small jars), all of my smaller squashes and different artwork or leaves our children have made or collected. The closed shelving unit (see the picture on the left) is only 9" deep and 24" wide. But in that space, the top holds all of my onions, garlic, rutabagas and ginger, while the bottom holds 50 pounds of potatoes.

Buying with Food Security in Mind

This chapter is really a bonus from a ~~cheap~~ practical woman. I am not a doomsday, "prepare for the end of the world" kind of person. I do realize there is always a possibility of our economy succumbing to depression, but I am not living in fear of it. My hard-learned motto is, "We'll deal with it when it comes."

That being said, I do have a lot of people to feed in our family (six! and they all want three meals a day! And snacks every hour!). Because of the nutrition benefits and lifestyle, we deeply strive to feed our children off the land as much as possible. An added bonus is the confidence we have in getting our food regardless of the economy.

But even with this striving, I still need to buy a fair amount of food from the grocery store. Maybe someday we'll need to buy very little, but I'm not at that point yet (as I said before six people, snacks every hour). So, I go to the grocery store ... and I'm going to let you in on a little-known secret. Grocery shopping with four children is ... is ... Overwhelming? Terrifying? Traumatizing?

Okay, okay, it's not that bad ... all the time. Sometimes it is. One time, I was pushing a cart nearly overflowing with groceries with a baby standing and trying to escape out of the cart, a little girl running around the aisle and a little boy screaming on the floor behind me because he was too hot and wanted his jacket off. My children really are well behaved so often, but the grocery store, the grocery store just brings out the worst in everyone sometimes.

So, with that in mind (and because of economy shifting, etc.), I strive to buy things that will last and allow me the ease to postpone a trip to the grocery store if so wanted (or needed) for my own sanity.

Here are some things I do.

Buy in Bulk

1. When I run out of my own potatoes and carrots, I buy in bulk from local farmers (50 lbs for potatoes and 10lbs for carrots usually). This is a much cheaper way of buying potatoes and carrots and buying this way means I really only need to buy carrots and potatoes (staples in our house) a few times a year.
2. Baking supplies. I buy most of my baking supplies in bulk from Costco. This again means I have less time between grocery shops. I am careful to only buy an amount which I know my family will use by the best-before-date, but I do appreciate not needing to get these things quite as often.
3. Meat. Josh has had a mean hunting streak which means we've had to buy a lot of our meat for the past while. Because we have so many people in our family (and a tight budget), I buy cheaper types of meat in bulk from a butcher shop. For instance, I buy large boxes of pork chops, bacon and chicken breasts which will last for many meals (especially when put in casseroles, soups and stews).

4. Rice. I love having lots of rice on hand. I can mix it with anything and it lasts for such a long time!

Buy with Sales

Before I get too far into this, I somewhat do and do not follow grocery store sales. I often wait for a product I need to go on sale before I buy it (like diapers), but I do not plan my meals around sales. I know I could do this and it might save our family more money, but honestly, I don't want to spend my time doing that. There are so many other things I would rather do! Also (my opinion here), grocery stores are like any other business in that they try to get you to buy more. Like, "You'll get one hundred bonus air miles if you buy ten boxes of cereal today!" When I first see those things, I think, "Oh yeah, what a good deal!" But then when I think about it a bit more, I realize I would be spending $50 on cereal I did not need to get 100 bonus air miles. I really weigh the pros and cons of sales and deals before I buy things because like I said above, I'm a ~~cheap~~ practical woman.

So now that you've heard my rant, this is one thing I do.

1. **Produce Sales.** When produce goes on super sale, I go wild. If apples are on some incredible super sale, I buy lots and turn them into applesauce or freeze them. I also keep an eye out for which produce is on sale when. Produce prices fluctuate a fair amount depending on if you are buying things when they are or are not in season.

I found bags and bags of "Less than Perfect" apples on sale for half price at the grocery store one week. Although many of the apples were close to going bad, I bought a bunch. I cut off the bad parts and made oodles of apple sauce (this is a 15-quart size pot).

We have also been learning how to make our own apple cider vinegar (which requires much patience), but has been quite fun. So not only did the apples give us apple sauce, they also gave us apple cider vinegar (and fed our chickens)!

This brings me to my next point

Buy in Season

I splurge on many fruits and vegetables when they are in season. Because we live in the North, I know it will cost a lot more to truck those fruits in later months (if we can even get them at all). So, when things are in season, I buy produce from food truck vendors so I can pickle, can or dry it and enjoy it without guilt all through the long winter months.

We bought pounds and pounds of cucumbers in the summer. Our family is wild about pickles so we decided to buy enough cucumbers to make around 45 jars of pickles.

We bought this pumpkin from a local farmer for $5 CAD in the fall. You probably cannot tell how huge this beast was in the picture. But let me tell you this. We got over 60 cups of roasted pumpkin from this ONE pumpkin!

A few last tidbits from a ~~cheap~~ practical woman

Here are some of my last tricks I have for going to the grocery store less and saving money.

1. Legumes. Lentils and dried peas are incredibly cheap and last a LONG time. Even canned beans are cheap. If I have sacks of lentils and beans in my cupboard, I know I can make meals that will fill up hungry bellies (even if I've run out of meat).

2. Skim Milk Powder. A few years ago, I was forced to cut my grocery budget nearly in half and when that happened, I discovered this trick. I make a small container of skim milk powder milk (like I mix the powder with water) and I use this in all my baking and even cooking. I don't love the taste of skim milk powder so I would rather not drink it, but no one can tell the difference when it is in a baked good. By doing this, I lessen how often I need to buy milk and save us money.

And there you have it. All of the tricks I use in helping me go to the grocery store as little as possible.

I was going to end this chapter here, but have had a change of heart after talking to my sister. When the coronavirus pandemic started hitting Canada in force, I got what I assume was cold. It's hard to know anything these days though so our family took the warnings to heart and started a two-week quarantine. My regular schedule of grocery shopping was meant to be a few days into our quarantine ... so taking all of this into account, our family went three weeks without getting any groceries. Our children still ate snacks throughout the day and we still ate three meals a day. But how did we do this?

If I had known we would have to go three weeks without groceries, I probably would have stocked up on things like cheese or skim milk powder, but I didn't know. So, we made due with what was in our house. This is what we did.

1. We rationed milk and juice (one cup of either/day/person) and switched to solely water when we ran out of those things. We also mixed store bought juice half and half with water to make it go farther.
2. I made a batch of baked oatmeal (using coconut milk) that lasted for quite a few breakfasts. I put apples from our freezer in and allowed the kids to add extra sugar (to make it more tempting for their picky palettes).
3. I buy a lot of plain yogurt and mix it with homemade jam for kids' breakfasts. Because we had so much yogurt, we switched the kids to having yogurt in their cereal instead of milk.
4. We made popcorn and had fruit teas for special snacks.
5. I made spaghetti with canned beans instead of meat.
6. I made a few batches of lentil soups (using potatoes, dried beans and other root vegetables) and we had that for lunch throughout the week.

7. We cooked a roast chicken or pork loin for dinner one night and used the leftovers to make casseroles the following days.
8. I always buy large amounts of fruits and veggies at the store (and usually replenish them before they go empty) so we had enough to last us (with some rationing) throughout our entire three weeks. When the fruit started getting low, we started subbing in snacks such as homemade canned fruit and homemade applesauce.
9. We ran out of kids' soap so we switched to teaching them how to use a bar of soap (without getting any in their eyes).
10. We rationed our eggs for mostly baking. (Our chickens were molting and were producing very few eggs/day).
11. I made sourdough bread as it required very little yeast (my sourdough starter has some issues - usually sourdough starter requires no yeast).
12. I also made artisan bread because it requires very few ingredients (flour, yeast, water and salt).
13. We ate rice or potatoes in some form often.
14. I let the kids snack on frozen peas or pickled veggies we had made in the summer.
15. The kids got to have half of a frozen banana for dessert (or a spoonful of honey).

It's not easy to skip going to the grocery store for three weeks straight while still raising a gaggle of children, but it is possible. Buying food this way, growing and foraging and preserving, taking care of chickens and bees - all these things actually work. Yes, I had to be creative, but the feat of going three weeks without getting any extra food sources and without doing any prior buying prep is a huge deal. It is testament to the fact that living this way works.

Conclusion

All that to say (refer back to all previous chapters), you are CAPABLE. You are ABLE. YOU CAN DO THIS!

Growing your own food, raising chickens and bees, hunting, foraging - you are able to do these things (even if you have a teeny tiny yard like Josh and Ashlee). Maybe it's going back to basics, but isn't that what the human race has been doing since the beginning of time? When it comes down to it, we've always had a few basic needs - shelter, water, food and companionship. A lot of other needs and wants can be put into that list, but that's always been (and always will be) the core.

Providing food for yourself and family will ALWAYS be a relevant and central need.

And you don't need to be completely reliant on the grocery store to take care of that need. You don't need to be pulled here and there by the economy. You can take care of this essential need in your own backyard no matter how small or large it happens to be.

Your yard - you - are capable of so much if you would simply try. Gardening, raising chickens and bees, these things are completely doable by **you** - even if you've only cared for a pet fish and a fake house plant. You may kill a few plants along the way. You will probably need to reach out to a knowledgeable friend (or google) for troubleshooting issues that come up. But all of this is

DOABLE. It is not scary and we guarantee, you will be absolutely astounded by all your yard and you are capable of doing.

Take the plunge. Start your journey of becoming a backyard homesteader.

Bonus Chapter

Beyond the Basics of the Backyard

{With Jamie Giesbrecht}

For those who are truly brave and for those who want to branch out even further, there are other, more advanced options in the animal husbandry realm. Let's take a look!

Rabbits

For many people, rabbits are pets. Rabbits are also a delicacy in many high-end restaurants. You may never have considered rabbits for consumption before, but here are some reasons you should give it a second thought:
- Rabbits are inexpensive and easy to raise
- Rabbits are quiet {not silent, as most people assume; they do make a very quiet sound in their throats}
- Rabbits are allowed within the city limits everywhere {keeping in mind, you would be expected to be keeping about the same amount as if you were keeping them as pets}
- They can be kept inside or outside, and there are many commercial housing options already available for them

While some people oppose consuming rabbits simply because of their prevalence as pets in our society, there are actually rabbit farms that exist for the sole purpose of bringing them to your dinner table!

If you decide to try to raise some meat rabbits, here's what to do:

1. Select a pre-made rabbit hutch, or create something out of what you have. Commercially, options range from inexpensive and plain to quite expensive and fancy.
2. Acquire feed. Just like with any other animal, I prefer to feed something that is recognizable rather than a pellet feed. Rabbits do very well on hay, so find a local farmer with a hay crop. Rabbits enjoy fresh kitchen scraps as well {please refer back to the kitchen scraps for chickens portion under 'Feeding Your Hens' - same rules apply}.
3. Supply fresh water. Rabbits can drink out of a traditional rabbit water bottle, which mounts to the side of their structure and has a nipple they suckle out of - this option creates little waste. They can also lap water out of a bowl.
4. Choose a rabbit, particularly, a larger breed. Rex rabbits, for example, are a considerably larger breed than the common dwarf rabbit. While all rabbits can be eaten, you will have more to serve with a large animal. Most rabbits are inexpensive to acquire.

5. Provide fun! Rabbits love to shred and chew paper and cardboard. This gives them something to do, and keeps them happy.
6. Raise your rabbit. As with most livestock, it is most common to raise and process a juvenile. And, just like with chickens, a crock pot will create a wonderful meal out of even the oldest of rabbits.

Small Acreages

People are often very surprised at what my husband and I are able to raise on 7 acres. Currently, we have a flock of 5 sheep {4 ewes and a ram}, about 50 birds {this includes chickens, ducks, geese, quail and turkeys}, 1 goat, a herd of horses {which actually includes 2 mules, some ponies and some miniature horses}, 3 dogs, 2 cats, and various indoor exotic pets. Some years, we also throw pigs in the mix, and we have done milking goats as well. We also have a garden, and 2 beehives. If you are considering moving to an out-of-town property, be encouraged that you can do a lot with a little.

Here are some key points to maximize your use of space:

- **Plan ahead.** It helps to map out your property on paper. Make a 'floor plan' for what you want to do. Consider your goals - what animals do you want to keep, for example. Try to plan the layout for maximum efficiency. Leave spaces for gates to open, equipment to get through, and allow for proper drainage. Think about a location for a central shed or mini barn for feed and equipment storage. Look at how far away pens will be from your water sources.

- **Think about multi-functional items.** Use fencing materials that will work for more than one animal. For example, pigs require hog panels to contain them well. These panels also work great for sheep and goats. Installing hog panels makes your pens work under many circumstances, and allows you to shift in the future.

Young pigs in a hog panel fencing system; the panels have been covered with chicken wire so the pen can also be used for poultry in the future, keeping them safe from predators {pigs would eat chickens, so they cannot live together}.

- **Provide comfort.** Animals should not be overly cramped. Animals need to have access to fresh water and shelter.

- **Build well.** Taking the time now to build something properly will save you time and money. It doesn't have to be fancy, but it shouldn't be falling apart.

- **Work with what you have.** We have used pallets - that we have acquired for free - as gates on many pens. This cuts down on costs, and is environmentally friendly. Repurpose items when possible.

- **Look at the possibility of using adjoining property.** We have the added benefit of being able to use an oil and gas wellsite behind our property to graze our horses all summer. This allows us to grass feed them, rather than needing to secure hay all year. Get permission, always - but don't be afraid to look into using easements or crown land {government property set aside for access to hydro, telephone or gas services, would be some examples}. Electric fences powered by solar panels allow you to easily set up on some of these alternative properties. Prices for this type of setup are falling, although it isn't considered inexpensive.

- **Crop share.** We are blessed enough to have property adjoining to my parents; our pasture adjoins their hay field. We cut, dry and bale the hay using their equipment and our time. In return, they allow us to take the portion of hay we need for our horses and sheep. They keep what they need, and sell the rest, making this a mutually beneficial situation. We have more than enough hay to feed our small farm, and the only cost is the time to process it. While it may seem daunting to ask someone about a crop share, it is well worth it. I know many people who have made such arrangements.

- **Rotate your pastures.** Because not everyone can find a nearby option to use for additional pasture, it is a good idea to make a series of fenced areas your grazing animals can use. When the grass gets low, move to the next section, BEFORE the grass is yellowing or eaten down to the dirt {otherwise regrowth is slow}. We also allow our horses to graze our driveway for 4-6 hours a day in early spring, before the wellsite behind us is dry, as a form of rotation.

A small acreage can produce an amazing amount of food for your family. We have placed our beehives in the hay field directly behind our house - with the permission of the owner - and our annual garden has given us plenty of fresh vegetables. Adding to our bounty are the abundant, wild saskatoon berry bushes on our property. We also have rose hips and wild strawberries. Although berries will vary from region to region, there is almost certainly something you can use on any acerage. Find a local that can help you safely identify the plants around you. Wild berries are an amazing source for jams, jellies, pies, and other baking.

Wild Saskatoons picked on our acreage.

If you have a small acreage, or have plans to purchase or rent one, many more possibilities open up as to what you can raise as far as animals, with varying degrees of difficulty. Let's take a look!

Pigs

One thing I love getting into my freezer every fall is some home-grown pork. The smoked hams and bacon all winter long are worth the work required to raise pigs. Because it is a bit more of an undertaking, let's look at some pros and cons.

Pros:

- Moderately priced to acquire, as far as livestock goes.
- Can eat a wide variety of kitchen scraps, including egg shells, dairy, and wheat products {on top of the fruit and veggie scraps}
- Requires little specialized care in the growing phase
- Puts a decent amount of quality meat in your freezer after 6-8 months - you can sell any that you don't need for some extra income .
- Some grocery stores allow farmers to pick up produce that hasn't sold and isn't yet spoiled, for their livestock. Pigs make good use out of this, and it will save you money.
- You can breed your sow {female pig} to sell piglets for extra income.

Cons:
- Most areas require compliance with a pig ear tagging program, which can be a nuisance and added cost for a small-scale farmer. These programs aim to ensure food safety and disease control, but require the purchase of tags and a tool to insert the tags in the ears of pigs. While tagging juvenile pigs is easy, tagging adult pigs is a real challenge due to their size and lack of controllability {pigs do not wear halters like some livestock, and don't respond to standing tied}. The farmer must also report, online, the movement of pigs off property {including the name and license plate number of the transporter, time the trailer left the yard, etc }.
- Meat must be processed in a government inspected facility if you would like to sell it.
- Pigs can be aggressive, and because they root with their noses underneath fences, they require a sturdy fencing system {such as hog panels or a post and beam fence, although this second option isn't good for keeping piglets in given their relatively small size as juveniles; they can be held in two

hands at birth, and aren't that much larger than a cat at weaning time}.

An example of a sturdy fencing system for older pigs - note the spacing between bars that would allow juveniles to escape.

A group of 4 weaned piglets {8 weeks of age} - note the small stature.

- Pigs can nip or bite hands that are put into their spaces, and can be difficult to move and load into trailers for transport; they do not herd like other, more docile livestock. Pigs have large teeth like a dog, and can seriously hurt you if they feel threatened.
- Pigs should be fed a proper ration with the right amount of protein {not from meat sources, if they are for human consumption} - this is very hard to do

124

consistently with just scraps {see note on 'Feeding Your Hens' - same rules apply}. Hog grower feed can be expensive.
- Breeding pigs means keeping or finding a boar for your sows. Sows aren't always great mothers, and can savage the piglets after they are born.

Pigs are actually quite intelligent, and prefer to eliminate their waste in one area. Contrary to popular belief that they are messy, I find they like their pen just so. If given hay or straw, they will take it by the mouthful to their bed area to make a warm place to sleep. They DO love mud, especially on a hot day, and will tip their water, if possible, to make mud. While raising pigs isn't for everyone, it might be a goal worth working towards.

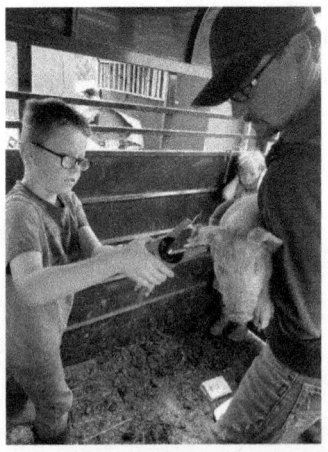

Ear tagging a young pig.

Goats for Milk and Meat

Goats are a dual-purpose animal. While some people raise them solely as pets, they can be a source of meat, and a source of milk. What an amazing thing, to have your own source of milk, right in your yard {at a much smaller size than a cow}. Some cities are starting to allow for the care of goats within the city limits. Goats have some unique behavior that can make this a challenge, whether you are on a farm, or in the city:

- Goats are incredible escape artists, and can thwart the best fencing system.
- Goats can jump extremely well, and walk on thin surfaces, such as the topline of a wooden fence. They enjoy jumping on and walking on vehicles.
- Goats are curious, to a fault. They taste test almost everything, and because they are dexterous, they get themselves into all kinds of trouble as far as what they eat, and what they destroy. They will pull at almost anything with their lips and teeth.
- Some goats are born "polled" {naturally hornless}, and some people will pay a veterinarian to remove goat horns. I have always felt that if the goat is born with horns, and we plan to raise them, we deal with the horns; they have them for a reason {the blood vessels in them help them regulate their temperature}. That being said, goats are not above ramming into your behind when you aren't looking! A goat that is not taught to behave and respect you from a young age is a goat that is bound to be

trouble. Goats that aren't taught not to ram can continually corner you and threaten to ram, or actually ram you into fences, buildings, etc. They think it's fun! This is a part of their genetic makeup, and how they deal with each other in the wild - they see you as just another goat to play with or put in line.
- Goats are vocal. They make a nasal snuffling sound that I quite enjoy, but they also bleat at a high volume, and often. Goats are personable, and may bleat upon seeing you, waiting for feed, or really, for any other reason they like. This is one reason that backyard goat keeping hasn't totally taken off yet.
- Male goats that are castrated are called whethers. Male goats that aren't castrated are called bucks, and they have some nasty habits. They urinate on their long facial beards, because that, apparently, attracts the ladies. This creates quite a smell, and if you have a light-colored goat, it looks just as bad as you can imagine.

Goats really are funny creatures, and kids {baby goats} are absolutely hilarious with their running and jumping antics. I quite enjoy them and I don't want to discourage you from giving them a try, if you're interested. Here are some of the great things about goats and some details on how to manage them:

- There is a variety of miniature goat, called the Nigerian Dwarf goat, which is much smaller than a traditional goat, that is a great milker. This is a good option for in town, or for anyone daunted by the size of full-sized milk goats. Remember, milking animals requires regular, consistent milking morning and night. If you take a break or go on vacation, the animal will get mastitis, and it is life-threatening, not to mention cruel. Some people will allow a kid goat to continue to nurse longer than normal to help ease the milking load. Does {female goats} need to be freshened {bred} in order to keep milk flowing, since milk production is induced by pregnancy and the delivery of kids. But this means allowing her to 'dry up' in order to be bred. You can count on about a ten-month lactation cycle, but as you can see, there is some work to this.

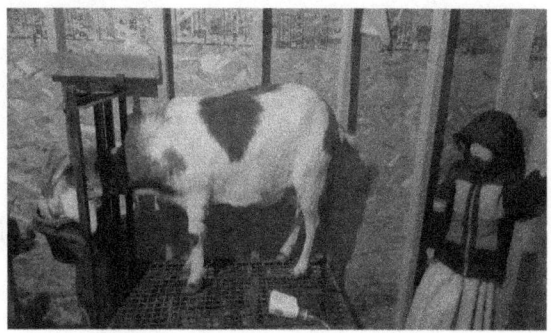

A doe on a milk stand, ready for milking.

- Goats are easy and inexpensive to feed. They do great on hay, which is very economical {when bought from a farmer - hay in pet stores is high priced}. They can be grazed on grass {be aware of spraying herbicides on grazing areas}, and they enjoy scraps {particularly greens, apple cores, etc.}. Goats are hearty, and can almost always find nutrients. They will eat shrubs and bushes, so watch your yard and garden. They LOVE to eat apples from the tree. Goats' milk, both in taste and color, are greatly affected by what they are eating. If they are eating willow bows, for example, the milk can taste woody; our milk goat, on hay, produced a lovely, sweet milk.

- Goats are intelligent, and companionable. They can wear a collar, and be taught to walk on a leash; they can also be taught to pull a small cart, or wear a pack. Perhaps this might help you with some work around the yard?

- You can make many products out of goat's milk, such as goat cheese, and soap. If you really want to dive deep into self-sufficiency, adding a goat to your property will help you immensely. The sale of goat's milk to the public is prohibited on a small scale {mostly because it isn't pasteurized by small-scale farmers}. Do invest in a good milk screen filter, and practice good hygiene when working with any animal products.

Using a milk filter. Filters are not as cheap as you would expect. They filter out the finest of particles.

- Goats produce a small, dry, pellet style stool. This is quite convenient, and easy to manage compared to other animals.

- There are commercial goat milking machines available at a moderate price to speed the process.

- Goat's meat {best raised from a meat breed, so you get more out of a carcass} is considered a delicacy in some areas. Raising your own meat means you know there are no hormones, antibiotics or other additives in it that you wouldn't want to feed your family.

- Sometimes, farmers sell kids {baby goats} that were a part of a triplet set that is too much for the doe. These babies need to be bottle fed. It is a lot of work, but nothing is nothing cuter than a bottle baby. What an experience!

Feeding a baby bottle goat.

Keeping a rejected kid inside during bad weather calls for some creativity.

Goat keeping is entertaining, and fruitful for your family. There are so many benefits to this interesting and valuable animal.

Sheep

Sheep are low maintenance, docile animals for the most part. Lamb is a versatile, desirable dish and a delicacy in many restaurants. If you are interested in adding this resource to your freezer, here is what you need to know:

- Sheep can graze in warmer months if you have the space, and do well on hay in winter. Provide a mineral supplement, especially for ewes you plan to breed.

- Sheep are not nearly as hard on fences as goats or cows {keep in mind, a breeding male, called a ram, will be very motivated to get through a weaker fence to females, though}.

- In many places, it is the law for all sheep to be ear tagged; it is illegal in some places for a sheep to leave your farm even to be taken to a veterinarian without an ear tag. Just like with pigs, the ear tag system is supposed to control disease outbreaks, and ensure food safety. Sheep ear tag programs are one of the strictest around.

- Keeping a ram to breed your ewes increases your costs {feed, medication, space}, and if you plan a breeding program, you will also have to plan to castrate young rams.

- Female sheep, called ewes, commonly give birth to twins, triplets, and even quadruplets. The more lambs born, the more likely one or more may need to be taken off the ewe and bottle fed, and that can be daunting for beginners.

- Sheep are easy to herd and move; their docile nature makes them a joy to work with.

- Hair sheep will shed out on their own in spring, but are much slower to mature to market weight. Traditional sheep with wool mature to market weight faster, but need to be sheared each spring.

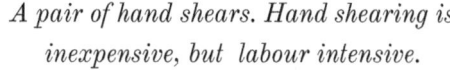

A pair of hand shears. Hand shearing is inexpensive, but labour intensive.

Below we use a goat milking stand for hand shearing. Electric shears can do a lot of damage if you aren't experienced with them; cuts can inadvertently happen even with hand shears.

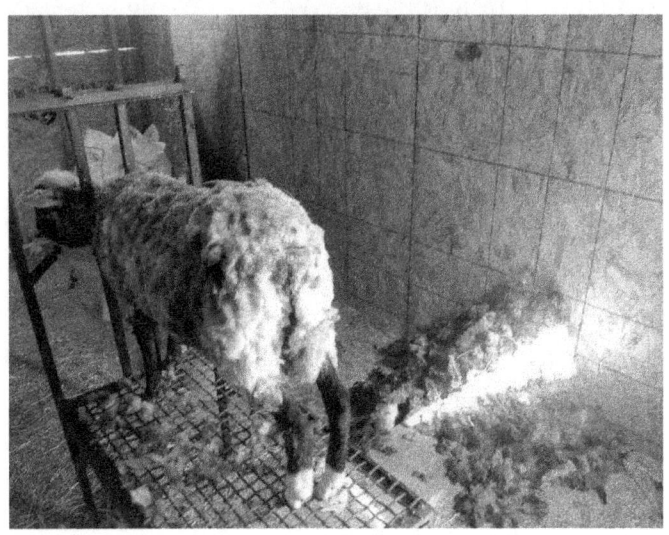

Trout

Yes, trout! Although fry {baby fish} suppliers can be difficult to find, this option has been around for years. We first stocked a pond with Rainbow trout about 30 years ago on our family farm when I was growing up. While this, again, is not an easy set-up, and isn't for everyone, here are some points to ponder:

- Fry can be transported home using some creativity - we used a decommissioned freezer filled with water.

- Fish will need a deep pond that does not freeze to the bottom in winter {solidly frozen pond means solidly frozen fish}. This depth will vary by region.

- The pond needs to be big enough to support the number of fish you want to introduce {ask your supplier for specific details} and expect some loss. Remember that fish are food for many birds and wild animals.

- Your pond will most likely require an aerator {which can be run inexpensively from a windmill, but is not inexpensive to acquire} to produce oxygen in the water, unless you are blessed enough to have some water flow through your pond from a creek.

- Your fish can eat bugs, algae, and, thankfully, leeches from your pond {meaning your pond will be much cleaner, and MUCH more fun to swim in with the leeches being taken care of - no one likes these blood suckers}, but you may need to supplement them with a pellet feed until they, and your pond, are established {and here is where it is important not to try to raise too many for the space you have}

Once you get this project going, you will not only have fish jumping in your own private mini lake on your own property, you will have yet another source of food at your fingertips.

Taking Self-Sustainability Seriously

While we are nearing the end of the book, there is one area of suggestion that I still want to address. While many of the suggestions here have been in regards to foraging, growing or raising your own food, you can go a step further. Let's look at some things you can do to truly sustain your home on a whole new level:

- If you live in town, where you can't raise your meat, consider asking a farmer to make a deal. Currently, we raise Cornish Giants {a fast-growing, meaty chicken} on our farm with our co-authors. Since they live in town, they can't do this, but we can. This is mutually beneficial, because we split the costs, and the work of processing when the chickens reach butcher weight. This can be done in raising any other farm animal for meat or wool or milk.

- Consider making as many things as possible yourself. Did you know that you can make your own yogurt? Your own soap? Your own wool products from the sheep on your farm? How many things could you stop buying from the store?

- Consider a wood fireplace or wood stove {please check provincial and federal regulations regarding certification, and your home insurance provider to ensure continued coverage}. Several years ago, my husband and I finally installed the wood fireplace that was in the floorplans for our house. We couldn't afford to put it in when we first built, and it wasn't cheap to put in when we finally did it. But ... our heating costs are ⅙ of what they used to be! We never buy firewood, although that option is out there. We look for friends that have trees they want removed from their yard {or old piles of firewood they don't plan to use}, neighboring properties that have cut down trees and want someone to haul them away, or deadfall on our own property. We haul it all home with a trailer, and then spend as little as an hour a day in summer working on it. Tyler cuts the logs into sections that fit into the wood splitter we invested in {I would recommend this; it saves a ton of time}. I enjoy splitting wood, as do some of our older children. So, we split and stack a little every day, until we are ready for winter. One particular evening, one of our children played her violin on the porch while I split wood and the other kids stacked. It was lovely! If you want to go a step even further, consider a true wood cookstove - the wood fuels the stove for cooking, and heats the house. True pioneer style!

Getting ready to unload an amazing score of wood we acquired from someone clearing their yard.

Rows of firewood, ready for winter.

- Going solar. This is a step we haven't taken yet, due to the cost of set up, but it is an appealing option.

- Collecting rainwater. We currently use rainwater for our livestock, flowers, and gardens {although we don't have enough collected at a time to use that as our only source}.

The beauty of a farm.

About the Authors

Jamie Giesbrecht

Photo credits to Blushin' Photography {Leanne Karlin}

Jamie Giesbrecht is a life-long farm girl who holds a diploma in Business Management from Northern Lights College, and is a Staff Storyteller and monthly contributor for Adoption.com. Additionally, you can find her articles in the '*Focus on Adoption*' magazine, as well as the '*Gospel Herald and the Sunday School Times*'. Her writing on adoption is described as elegantly emotional, beautifully crafted, honest, and raw in all the right places.

Jamie is married to her high school sweetheart and best friend, Tyler. Together, they are passionate about adoption and foster care, as well as living off the land. Jamie is a stay-at-home mama to 3 adopted and 2 biological children who run wild on their small farm in rural, Northern Canada. When she is not homeschooling the kids, Jamie can be found seeking adventures with her family in the Yukon and Northwest Territories, hunting, fishing, camping, or trail riding the horses to town. Her hobbies include cross stitching, reading, and horseback riding as often as she can.

Josh and Ashlee Kirschner

From years of insatiable reading and study, Josh and Ashlee's writing is honest, informative and varied. While Ashlee earned a Certificate of Horticulture from Thompson Rivers University in 2012 and WWOOFed in Hana, Hawaii, Josh studied and practiced Joinery through the British Columbia Institute of Technology. After years of work in their respective trades, they decided to take the plunge and start both a landscaping and a woodworking business.

Although both are now working their dream jobs, they still have an insatiable desire to learn to live off the land and be in nature. So, while raising four wild children may keep them busy, you will often find them out working in their yard or hiking a gorgeous trail somewhere. In between work, kid and outside time, you'll find them writing, doing a puzzle, watching *Perry Mason* or *The Office*, or reading until the wee hours of the night. Learn more about them at ashleekirschner.com

Other Books by Ashlee Kirschner

Longevity: Creating and Sustaining a Lifelong Faith

After a time of silence and introspection, ashlee felt compelled to write her story - full of her failings, victories and most of all her encounters with a real, active God. Bearing testimony to the logical reasons for God and yet delving deeply into struggles with Biblical passages, it is both personable and informative.

"This book is one of the most beautifully honest books I've read. Ashlee has a way with words that speak so much life and truth. In reading this book, I had my faith confirmed through extraordinary apologetics. I had my eyes opened to the likeness of my struggles. I had my heart opened to the faithfulness of a God so great." Amazon Reviewer

"This book was a very raw and honest glimpse into a life of faith and a journey in the author's relationship with Christ. I wish there were more people who were willing to be so vulnerable and open with their stories. I was challenged and moved. Whether you're just starting out in your journey with Jesus or have been on the road for a long time, this book will be an encouragement to your heart." Amazon Reviewer

"The author shares her story of growth in such a way that is beautifully unguarded and gives a fresh take on who God is and who I am." Amazon Reviewer

"I wasn't sure what to expect with this book, but once I started reading, I was captivated. It's beautifully written, yet real, raw and relatable. I feel there are valuable takeaways for any person. I'm getting some more copies for gifts to friends to offer them encouragement & hope as it did for me." Amazon Reviewer

Notes and Recipes